DEANNA FARNETI CERA

COSTUME
JEWELLERY

Foreword by Jean Appleton

Founding Chairman of the Society of Jewelry Historians, U.S.A..

ANTIQUE COLLECTORS' CLUB

© 1995 Arnoldo Mondadori Editore S.p.A., Milan
This edition published 1997

ISBN 185149 265 8

British Cataloguing-in-Publication Data
A catalogue record for this book is available from the British Library

The right of Deanna Farneti Cera to be identified as author of this work has
been asserted in accordance with the Copyright, Designs and Patents Act, 1988

Printed and bound in Spain by Artes Gráficas Toledo, S.A.
D.L.: TO: 130-1997

CONTENTS

PREFACE

It is startling to realize that less than two decades ago a book on the history of what is known as costume jewelry did not exist. The subject was thought to be too large, even disorderly. The revered name of Chanel was a monument in a vast uncharted area, with possibly a dozen other names in America and Europe known only to cognoscenti, savvy dealers, and the few collectors who had nourished their passion through fashion collecting. In trunks, closets, and auctions these jewels were surfacing. With the auction in New York in 1987 of the collection of Diana Vreeland, the near-mythical fashion doyenne, and the subsequent sale at Drouot in Paris 1991, costume jewelry emerged as the decorative "art star" it is.

Vintage, collectible, faux, or fantasy, the nomenclature can be debated, but what such objects have in common are joie de vivre, wit, opulence, and above all daring. Daring in the sense that untrammeled creativity is possible when cost and inventory are not of prime consideration. We need think only of how, from earliest times, makers of costume jewels were inventive in the use of nonprecious materials; consider the Roman matron sporting glass-inlay rings and bangles of amber and bone, the spectacular multihued faience in Egyptian amuletic pieces, the strass that glittered by candlelight at Versailles soirées. Later it was pinchbeck, coated iron, pyrite, and cut steel, and in the twentieth century exploding technology brought plastics and mass production.

Costume jewelry is the mirror of our sociological history between the two great wars. In it we see the liberation of women by Chanel, their subsequent feminization by Dior, the power of the cinema, and the communications and pictorial revolution that produced the motor-driven, mechanized uni-world we live in today.

Above all, the removal of economic restraints created the first and only truly democratic art form in the symbiosis between fashion and fantasy jewelry. From the street to the palace and back again, we have documented evidence of the passage of costume jewelry and its universality. In costume jewelry anything is possible, even borrowing the strange whimsy of the Surrealists, or the oversized scale of Pop, or duplicating the prized techniques of precious jewelry.

The great foursome of Schlumberger, Verdura, Schiaparelli, and Chanel had an incestuous relationship with the arts which unleashed playful, witty ideas and set the pace for the succeeding generations of couturiers. As the garments were transformed from the great days of opulence to meet the demands of modern living, so the jewels changed and important venues shifted.

Deanna Farneti is once again an invaluable guide to images catalogued in precise detail, which are representative of the twentieth century's most distinguished examples. Cascading across these pages are images of beauty and imagination demonstrating the human urge to seize the natural and transform it with mind and hand, using a cornucopia of materials to execute dreams into stunning images.

—Jean Appleton
Society of Jewelry Historians

Jewelry Selection Criteria

A book of this nature has involved a great deal of research into unexplored areas and some careful consideration for choosing jewelry. I have tried to select significant examples from three categories of nonprecious ornaments: those that were conceived from the beginning as autonomous decorative objects, disconnected from styles in jewelry; those that best represent the evolution of taste and technique; and those that are recognized as noteworthy documents of an era and endowed with artistic value. With a few rare exceptions, selection was limited to objects of personal decoration, such as pins, necklaces, bracelets, and earrings.

The period under consideration extends from the beginning of the century up to the end of the sixties. Following the liberating 1960s, the passion for decoration expanded to the whole body: from beads for the hair to ornaments for shoes. Some gaps will be obvious, due to difficulties in finding material or to the impossibility of making it public. In fact, the archives that can be consulted are few, the sources scattered, and the memories of witnesses often vague. Only rarely are there traces of the prototypes or originals from the manufacturing firms. For example, in Italy the eagerly awaited Museo del Bijou di Casalmaggiore, which will present examples of Italian costume jewelry produced from the beginning of the century to 1950, is still being readied. The majority of the published objects are signed or identified. Attribution of a nonprecious ornament is easy when the object is signed with the name of a manufacturer or a maker that has been known since its establishment and about whom there are abundant biographies. Examples include Trifari, Napier, Monet, Schiaparelli, and Chanel. The patent number stamped on the back of some objects made in America can also be used to determine the name of the designer or maker. In fact, all the documentation relating to the granting of a license for both inventions (patent) and designs (design patent) is in the U.S. Patent Office in Washington, D.C.

The legal stamp (lit. punch) is a help in the attribution of objects made of silver. This mark is obligatory in the Nordic countries, England, Germany, and in France where legislation calls for two stamps, one for the quality of the metal and another showing the maker's initials. Silver legislation in Italy and the United States does not require a maker's stamp, but only the quality of the metal ("800" in Italy; "sterling," corresponding to 925-thousandths silver, in the United States).

Assigning a precise authorship and history to unsigned objects is more difficult. However, they are often worthy of being made public because of their beauty and possible historic significance. For some of the unsigned ornaments published in this book, accumulated experience and the relevant research carried out for this occasion were of no use. Although some pieces can be ascribed to a certain cultural area and to a given era because of their form and technique of production, they continue to lack a definitive attribution. Nonetheless, we have decided to publish them, with the aim of encouraging further research and conclusions. The name of the designer and the maker are indicated only when known. "Unidentified" means that the engraved letters are either illegible or unidentifiable.

We have reproduced the marks as they appear engraved or stamped on the objects, which will be helpful to collectors and dealers. Also useful, we hope, is the chronological arrangement of objects, which not only helps to date an object but to relate it to other cultural artifacts from the same period. The jewelry is in chronological order by style and, where possible, by country.

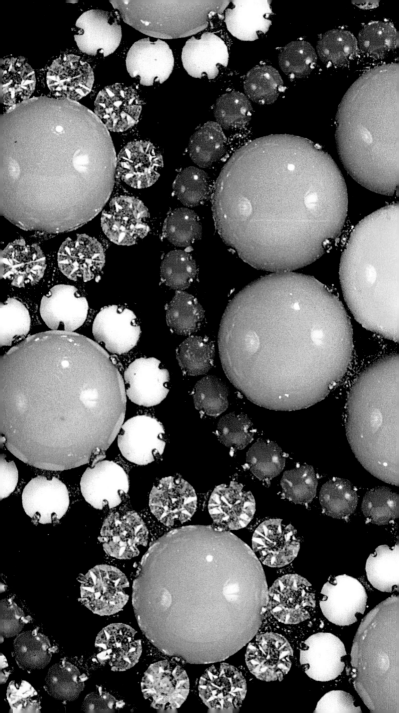

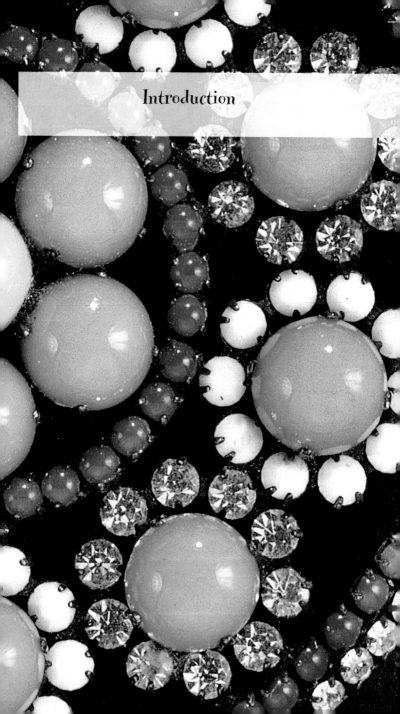

Introduction

Drawing of a demi-parure.
Miriam Haskell, New York,
c. 1935. Pasteboard,
tempera, purpurin, and
marcasite.

Costume Jewelry

The term costume jewelry (origi-nally from the French *bijou fantasie*) is understood to mean personal ornaments (pins, necklaces, bracelets, earrings) created from a wide range of ordinary and semiprecious materials. They are decorative elements that, in and of themselves, have an ephemeral function, destined to fade away when fashion changes.

Three Categories of Costume Jewelry

As in the clothing industry where there are three levels of quality, haute couture, prêt-à-porter or ready-to-wear, and mass produced, so in the field of non-precious ornaments a distinction must be made between *bijou de couture* (an accessory designed for high fashion), costume jewelry (for ready-to-wear), and low-cost trinkets—mass produced, distributed in department stores, and marketed to a wide audience.

Bijou de couture originated with the birth of haute couture around 1910 in France and made a name for itself in the twenties and thirties with Chanel and Schiaparelli. From France it spread to America and to the rest of Europe. A piece of jewelry was associated with the name of the couturier who paired it with an outfit, even if the couturier had not come up with the original idea for the jewelry. Thus, we say "Chanel, Schiaparelli, Balenciaga, Dior jewelry," and so forth.

Costume jewelry can be executed in an abundance of humble and semiprecious materials: metal, silver, glass, synthetic stones, marcasite, crystal, ceramics, mother-of-pearl, imitation pearls, wood, leather and chamois, feathers, fur, cork, raffia, rope, fabric, trimmings, shells, seeds, leaves and flowers, semiprecious stones (coral, quartz, peridot, turquoise), enamel; and in the past,

Page from a costume
jewelry catalogue, c. 1935.

fossils, horn, bone, tortoise shell, ivory, elephant hide, rubber, even insects. In the majority of cases, these materials are skillfully worked by hand.

From the 1950s on, a *bijou de couture* is generally signed with the name of the couturier who selected it for one of his outfits and had it made in limited quantities in a craftsman's workshop outside the designer's own atelier. Bearing a specific style that can be traced back to a particular stylist, it evolved over the course of the designer's collections.

Costume jewelry of medium to high quality, destined for a very wide audience, issues from specialized manufacturers and craftsmen's workshops and is often conceived by important designers and inspired by current fashion trends. It is almost always cast in molds and finished by hand. The amounts produced vary: hundreds of pieces in Europe and thousands in the United States, which has an extremely vast market for this type of jewelry. Manufacturers sell these objects under their own names, either directly or through distributors, in specialized shops or clothing boutiques. In America, they are mostly sold in specialty stores or in luxury department stores.

Patriotic pin in the shape of a "V," a wish for victory. Joseph Mazer & Co., New York, c. 1941. Cast in gilded metal, rhinestones, and red and blue baguettes. Stamped: Mazer.

research. Millions of women of all social classes wear costume jewelry. Today, as yesterday, this kind of trinket performs numerous social functions: a colorful pin adorns a woman who, for a few cents, has given in to a whim; a red Bakelite heart comforted a woman whose husband or fiancé had gone to war; a "V" in the red, white, and blue colors of the American flag, pinned to the lapel, expressed the hope of victory for the soldiers who had enlisted to defend Europe against Nazism; a small Christmas tree brooch gladdens the holiday season; a pin in the shape of a name can be an endorsement for a political candidate; a crossed red ribbon, worn in recent years by millions of people, sends a message of solidarity to those suffering from AIDS.

These specialized businesses and shops sometimes commission pieces originally put out by the fashion houses. In these cases, the jewelry will be distributed to the various markets under the name of the actual fashion house. Whereas *bijoux de couture* creates fashion or anticipates it, costume jewelry follows behind as a driving force.

Costume jewelry lines designed for broad distribution are produced in thousands of units, in the majority of cases by assembling preexisting pressed components, and are sold in popular department stores nationwide.

This kind of ornament is an integral part of American culture. It springs from current events or from the political and social topics of the day rather than from formal

Jewelry Identification

Jewelry belonging to the aforementioned three categories may or may not be signed. *Bijoux de couture*, created beginning in the twenties in Europe and from the thirties to the middle of the fifties in the United States, are not signed. The couturiers who had them made and sold them either in their boutiques or through their exclusive distributors (Poiret, Chanel, Schiaparelli, Adrian) were too famous to think that they needed to identify what were merely simple accessories to their outfits. As a result, many of these objects were never signed. It is

Advertising poster for
Trifari jewels.

even harder to imagine that jewelry being signed by their makers, who were without a doubt very skillful craftsmen but too modest to presume to affix their names.

In the majority of cases, American costume jewelry, produced beginning in the thirties in multiple copies by large specialized businesses, is signed. However, Miriam Haskell's jewelry, made entirely by hand and therefore comparable to *bijoux de couture*, was, with rare exceptions, not signed until the early fifties. Both American and European low-cost costume jewelry, executed in materials other than silver, are generally not signed.

Attribution of unsigned *bijoux de couture* arises from knowledge of the subjects and recognition of the workmanship. In part, this knowledge can be acquired by looking at the magazines of the

era, where designers' outfits were often published complete with accessories.

In the majority of cases of unsigned costume jewelry, typology combined with workmanship suggests the attribution. But sometimes the identifying element may be the clasp of a necklace, the use of certain stones in a particular shape, or the application of a specific enameling technique.

Appraisal

The price of a jewel is determined by the characteristics that distinguish the category to which it belongs. It will vary according to whether the product is in style or out of fashion, signed or anonymous, the work of an artisan or one of a series, innovative or banal, of good or poor workmanship, durable or easily damaged, well preserved or in very poor condition, rare or easily found. Going back over time, since their very origin, nonprecious ornaments have never been low-cost, as their creation, in any case, has always required specialized labor. Therefore, it has always been expensive enough to be exclusive.

In our own time, the same rule applies: *bijoux de couture* and good-quality costume jewelry, even vintage jewelry, continue to be luxury products, therefore expensive, and destined for those who can afford to follow the whims of fashion.

13

INTRODUCTION

Pin in the shape of a bird in flight. Alfred Phillippe for Trifari, United States, c. 1935. Cast in rhodium-plated metal and pavé rhinestones. Stamped: Trifari: Robin Feldman Collection, New York. Here is a beautiful example of the use of rhinestones in the years when "white" jewelry in platinum and diamonds predominated.

Costume Jewelry Components

The individual elements that make up costume jewelry are called components. They are available on the market in thousands of models, or they can be made to order for use in exclusive products.

Components are divided into two broad categories: functional (settings, links, clasps, spacers, pins) and ornamental (pendants, beads, stones, tubes, letters, numbers, etc.). Components can be made of metal, glass, or plastic. Alloys used for jewelry components contain a variety of metals in different proportions, the majority of which melt at low temperatures. Among them are copper, zinc, tin, lead, aluminum, and silver. Components made of glass include an extremely wide range of products: imitation stones for mounting, beads for stringing, and paste in an infinite variety of shapes and colors, obtained from pulverized glass and melted and cast in molds.

Imitation stones (colored glass simulating natural gems such as ruby, sapphire, and emerald) are of major importance in the history of costume jewelry. But the clear rhinestone, a substitute for the diamond, is without a doubt the principal element in nonprecious ornaments. Thanks to this faceted glass stone—which is both extremely brilliant, because of a mirrorlike amalgam on the bottom that increases the refraction of light, and hard enough to be cut in a thousand ways and mounted in an infinity of shapes—the art of jewelry became a mass phenomenon, especially in the twentieth century.

The most versatile of all materials used by the creators of costume jewelry is plastic and its derivatives. Practically unknown until the beginning of the twentieth century (it first appeared in the middle of the nineteenth century), today plastic can be worked in the solid, semisolid, and liquid states, thus presenting a challenge to jewelry makers. The plastics currently employed in the costume jewelry industry derive from six basic substances: cellulose, vinyl, phenol, ammine, casein, and nylon.

Those plastics which, when subjected to high temperatures, can be repeatedly softened and cooled to take on a desired shape (for example, celluloid, acrylic

Buckle. Germany, early
1900s. Paste and silver-
plated metal. Not stamped.

substances, and rhodoid) are called thermoplastics. However, plastics that once formed cannot be reliquified and reshaped are said to be thermoset, such as Bakelite, all of the phenolic resins, and galalith. Naturally, this second type of plastic requires more careful and precise workmanship, given that once it is formed there is no way of making changes.

Two methods are employed for producing plastic components: compression molding (for forming thermosetting materials) and injection molding (for thermoplastic materials—polystyrene, acetate, acrylic—used particularly in forming beads for stringing).

Metallic alloy components, whether functional or ornamental, are also made according to two basic techniques: casting and dieing. Casting is a method of molding substances that have been liquified by heat. The liquified substances are poured into a hollow matrix that reproduces the pattern in reverse. Once cooled, they give rise to a copy of the same in positive. The other technique utilized for making components is dieing, a method of molding utilizing dies operated by presses. Each die is composed of two parts, an upper and a lower. The force of the press cuts and shapes the sheet in-serted between these two parts into the desired design.

How Costume Jewelry is Created

Who are the creators of costume jewelry? People from the most diverse cultures and backgrounds. Naturally, first place belongs to those who have specific training in this field: artisans, goldsmiths, jewelers, and accessories designers. Among these, Fulco Santostefano della Cerda, Duke of Verdura, and Jean Schlumberger are the most important figures. They began their careers as designers of costume jewelry in the thirties, the former for Chanel, the latter for Schiaparelli. But they reached the height of their success later on as creators of precious jewelry in an unmistakable, highly individual style. An exhibition dedicated to Schlumberger's work was held at the Musée des Arts Decoratifs in Paris in the fall of 1995, and his collection continues to be produced and sold by Tiffany. Fulco di Verdura's business, based in New York, is still in operation.

A determining factor in a designer's career is the role of mentor provided by their employer. Jean Clément's story is exemplary. In 1927 the young painter, trained at the École des Beaux Arts in Paris and with a degree in chemistry,

was taken on at a very
young age as a designer
of accessories by Elsa
Schiaparelli.

Clément combined
his innate taste and
ability in working with
plastic materials with
the ingenious ideas
provided by Madame
Schiaparelli. He creat-
ed sophisticated, even
ironic objects (hand-
bags, buttons, belts
and costume jewelry)
of unforgettable beauty
that are worthy of the Schiaparelli
mark. One of his plastic necklaces,
with multicolored insects set as if
they were gems, has for years been
part of the permanent collection
of the Brooklyn Museum in New
York. Important personalities who
were not specifically trained in the
art of jewelry making also devoted
themselves to costume jewelry.
Renowned artists such as Dalí,
Giacometti, Man Ray, and Cocteau
created jewelry and accessories
for Schiaparelli; Calder designed
jewelry with a spiral motif, in
brass, silver, and gold. Many couturiers, among them Emilio Pucci,
Carosa, and Valentino, not only
commissioned their costume jewelry but also designed some of it
themselves.

Gianfranco Ferré is the proprietor of one of the most prestigious lines, not only for "Made in
Italy," but also for French couture

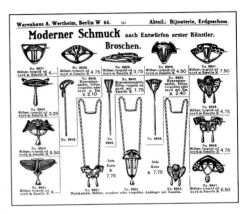

since he began signing the Dior
collections in 1989 to ever-increasing success. After earning
his degree in architecture, Ferré
began his career in 1969, working
for years on the production of accessories and costume jewelry.

Immediately after World War
II, gentlewomen of the aristocracy
dedicated themselves to creating
nonprecious accessories. Among
them are Baroness Luciana Aloisi
de Reutern (in art, "Luciana"),
Simonetta Visconté, and Costanza
Piccolomini (in art, "Copic").

Finally, some individuals who
began their careers as simple artisans in the field of nonprecious
ornaments rose to the status of
artists during their lifetimes: Line
Vautrin in France, Giorgio Vigna
in Italy, Sam Kramer and Ed
Wiener in America.

Clara Calamai, a famous ac-
tress of the forties, presented her

INTRODUCTION

Geometric pin. Costanza Piccolomini Mucchi, Milan, c. 1960. Rock crystal, tourmalines, pink and white quartz in an openwork setting on a silver mount. Stamped: Copic, Collezione Setti Carraro, Milan. Costanza Piccolomini Mucchi was a Milanese noblewoman who created "artistic jewelry" in very limited editions, usually 150 copies of each piece.

first collection of costume jewelry in Florence in 1960. These jewels were so highly regarded that their appearance was worthy of mention in *Women's Wear Daily*.

The initial idea for a piece of costume jewelry is first expressed in a drawing. The designer, aware of the market sector he is trying to reach, chooses the most appropriate solution for creating a new object whose final cost is within reach of the potential buyer.

Until the advent of the industrial age, jewelry was made by artisans and the same person attended to all the processes involved in creating the object, from the initial design to the final mounting of the stones. Therefore, the cost of the jewel was not determined as much by the cost of labor, which was more or less the same for all jewelry of the same type, as by the value of the materials used.

Beginning in the final decades of the nineteenth century, mechanization largely replaced hand working, especially in the field of nonprecious objects. The first industries dedicated to the manufacturing of components for precious and costume jewelry were founded in France, Germany, and the United States—in particular in Providence, Newark, and in New York State. Even today, Framex, established in 1866 in French Jura, is one of the most well known of these companies.

These businesses have thousands of semifinished models on hand, ranging from contemporary shapes to scores of new editions of designs from the past. This array allows the maker of finished products to have at his disposal not only exclusive, made-to-order components, but also thousands of prefabricated components. Today therefore, the price of a jewel, in contrast with the past, is determined above all by the cost of manpower, rather than the cost of the materials used to make it.

Designers can execute their ideas in two ways, the first being less costly than the second: he or she can assemble pre-existing components or choose shapes and motifs created exclusively for his or her firm, limiting the use of ready-made components to the functional elements only (clasps, spacers, pins, and so forth). Some designers can make totally creative jewelry

Pin. Emma Ivancich, Capri, Italy, c. 1960. Pasted spheres "sewn" on a metallic gallery on which are glued leaf-shaped elements in mother-of-pearl, cabochon-cut carnelian stones, Venetian glass beads, tinsel, and metallic, open-work, small findings. In the center of the piece, a balance wheel from a watch is used as a decorative element, with a round agate stone set in the middle.

using only preexisting components, sometimes even borrowing from related fields such as watchmaking. In the United States where the components industry is among the richest in the world in terms of shapes and finishes offered, there is a highly sought-after professional figure called a "manipulator."

With a combination of imagination and creativity, humor and awareness, irony and impudence, collective memory and personal learning, this individual selects and arranges ready-made components to their best advantage. Many of the famous subjects and shapes of American jewelry, now considered to be highly desirable, came from the hands of these "conjurers" who employed serial components in unusual ways, giving birth to innovations of reliable commercial success and undeniable taste.

From the design that provides the relevant technical information for the object, the modeler constructs a prototype, or original pattern, sticking as closely as possible to the instructions received. Once approved by the firm's art director (in craftsmen's workshops one or perhaps two people serve as creator, designer, modeler, producer, art director), the pattern becomes a part of the season's collection and the basis for making the shapes necessary for casting and molding the dies for individual components that are not already made. When the manufacturing of the components for a specific object is finished, production begins.

The components, either preexisting or specifically created for

Jewelry designed by Carosa for his 1960 summer collection. Private collection, Milan.

the article, are joined together to form the desired object. After the article is formed, it is first immersed in special baths that clean it and protect it against oxidation, then in a nickel-based polish bath. Next, the object is galvanized by immersion in baths containing precious metals (gold, silver, rhodium) in order to give it the desired coloring. Continued hardness is assured by covering the object with a protective lacquer and heating it at high temperatures to permanently fix the new coating.

The last procedure is mounting (manually pressing a stone into a setting with prongs that, once bent, hold the stone in place) or pasting the rhinestones and imitation stones into the preformed cavities in the metallic body.

Edwardian, Arts and Crafts, and Art Nouveau Jewelry

At the beginning of the century, women had already set off on the road to emancipation: some

women worked, some traveled, some played sports. A few of them were the muses who inspired great artists, and others embodied the myth of the femme fatale. Actresses and singers influenced public taste through their appearances in public and on the stage. Love stories, passions, and crimes unreeled amid silks and white crinolines on which garland-style ornaments, as delicate and light as lace, stood out. There were very few diamonds in the cascades of jewels worn by courtesans and ladies of easy morals, but plenty of rhinestones skillfully mounted in elaborate settings like those used for fine platinum jewelry.

The death of Queen Victoria obliged women of the aristocracy to observe a period of mourning, not only in their dress, but in their jewelry which, according to etiquette, had to be either all black or all white. The wife of King Edward VII was Queen Alexandra, a woman whose delicate beauty was accentuated by tight-waisted dresses that made her appear even more lean and regal. Queen Alexandra chose to wear white jewels: pearls and diamonds either falling in cascades or in tight collars (known as *colliers de chien*), which emphasized her statuesque elegance. With her image in mind, working women and moderately well-off women showed off small silver and rhinestone ornaments depicting animals, gazebos, pagodas, shrubs, flowers, baskets, and half-moons, some of superb workmanship, others more ordinary.

In the cultivated and cosmopolitan art world of the late 1890s, a new style, Art Nouveau, made its appearance. Its sinuous lines were applied not only to jewelry and ornaments, but also to architecture and everyday articles. The new style presented itself as an expression of the culture that privileged quality of artisanship over that of the decline in taste of the emerging industrial mass production.

An explanation for the swift, diffuse spread of the principles of Art Nouveau must be sought in the climate of cultural renewal that accompanied the growth of industrialization and the ensuing development of the middle class. Technical innovations and individual artistic experiments were quickly broadcast throughout Europe and the United States by international exhibits, newspapers,

and fashion magazines, which helped to promote a substantially uniform style, varied of course by local factors and situations.

The antecedent for the flourishing of Art Nouveau was the English Arts and Crafts movement, founded by William Morris and a few of his disciples who esteemed the manual labor of artisans over the loss of individual artistry caused by mechanized industrial production. With the goal of creating a popular art form that would appeal to the masses, William Morris opened a small firm in 1861 that produced and distributed objects made entirely by hand. Further associations and schools, inspired by medieval models, were founded with the aim of encouraging artisans. Exhibits and conferences followed. William Morris and his disciples believed that the new art should be based on the intrinsic quality of any material, from whose substantially unchanged essence beauty would spring forth.

Thus, in jewelry making, silver was preferred to gold. Cabochon-cut and raw stones were more admired than faceted ones. The irregularities of Baroque pearls, mother-of-pearl, and semiprecious stones were accorded a new value. A central theme of Arts and Crafts jewelry was the rediscovery of enamel as a nonprecious material through which an artisan could express himself. In the field

Bracelet and necklace.
Maker unknown, England,
late 1890s. Jet (fossil coal).

of nonprecious ornaments, humble objects, whose composition and finishing was deliberately crude rather than highly finished, emerged from this style. Hammered motifs, burnishing, engraving, and sharp edges abounded.

Kolomon Moser and Josef Hoffman established the Wiener Werkstätte (1898–1933), a community of Viennese artisans based on the principles of the English Arts and Crafts movement. The jewelry and nonprecious objects made by the Wiener Werkstätte were abstract in shape, geometric and linear in design, and often in delicate bicolor tones.

The initiatives of the Arts and Crafts movement and its disciples did not, however, have the anticipated result of creating art for the masses. By refusing to use machines, the entirely handmade products turned out to be fairly expensive and therefore inevitably accessible only to the elite. Nonetheless, the Arts and Crafts movement, which also spread to the United States during this period, was among the first art movements to confront the issue of the relationship between artistic content and industry, an issue that has yet to be totally resolved.

In continental Europe, Art Nouveau played a role similar to that of the Arts and Crafts movement in England and elsewhere, as the objects made according to the tenets of this new style could only be made by hand.

In France, René Lalique (1860–1945), the indisputable genius of the Art Nouveau period, created a new language of jewelry making,

Banded bracelet. France, early 1920s. Flexible links in silver- and gold-plated metal, forming a pattern of alternating lozenges. The center is a glass-paste scarab in golden-green shades. This jewel illustrates the Egyptian revival that occurred after the discovery of the tomb of King Tutankhamen.

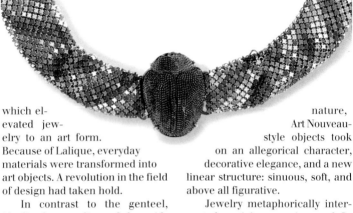

which elevated jewelry to an art form. Because of Lalique, everyday materials were transformed into art objects. A revolution in the field of design had taken hold.

In contrast to the genteel, idealized naturalism of the mid-nineteenth century, the stylistic elements of Art Nouveau jewelry are based on an intimate, poetic relationship with nature. Nature became associated with femininity and took on a symbolic quality.

A new awareness of Japanese and Chinese art, which displayed great subtlety and sensitivity, also influenced the artists of the time. The first exhibition of Japanese art in the West was held in London in 1854. In 1862, the Japanese were invited to the International Exhibition, also in London. The strength and precision of the woodcuts, the color of the enamels, the metal working, inlaying, and lacquers deeply impressed European artists and collectors. This exotic breath of fresh air gave new life to the largely academic realism of Western art.

Through direct contact with nature, Art Nouveau-style objects took on an allegorical character, decorative elegance, and a new linear structure: sinuous, soft, and above all figurative.

Jewelry metaphorically interpreted eroticism, passion, and *fin de siècle* decadence, using various motifs. Botanical motifs such as a soft bud, languid lily, and diaphanous bellflower represented birth, death, and rebirth. Other forms appeared, such as a delicate butterfly, evoking the fleeting nature of beauty, or a scarab, the Egyptian symbol for the life cycle. Mermaids, landscape motifs, and above all interpretations of the female form, which could be sensual, melodramatic, languishing, or sometimes stylized, were adapted.

Traditional rhinestone pavé jewelry continued to be produced during this period. But the great success of paste and plastics simulating coral, ivory, horn, and tortoise shell illustrates the abandonment of old traditions in those years. Gems and hard metals were no longer required. Jewelry was prized for its smoothness and fluidity, as well as for the value of the materials used to make it. Artisans used traditional enameling techniques (cloisonné and champlevé) as well as newer methods of application, such as *plique à jour*, which was introduced in France around 1900.

At the same time that artisans were experimenting with enameling techniques, designers were also reevaluating the decorative potential of another traditional medium—glass. Thanks to its natural properties, glass was well suited to the formal tenets of Art Nouveau. Talented glass artists like Emile Gallé (1846–1904) and René Lalique dedicated themselves to working with this material.

Women also actively participated in the renewal of the art of jewelry making. In the July 1, 1908 edition of *Femina*, Jeanne Perrin discussed two female artisans, Louise Baudin and Myto René Jean, who had exhibited their semiprecious jewelry at the Salon. Baudin possessed a distinctive modern style, using tin and copper to set off an abundance of topaz, lapis lazuli, malachite, quartz, Baroque pearls, and chrysoprase. Jean, a student of the enameler Paul Grandhomme, created jewelry fashioned from antiqued silver, lapis lazuli, and aventurine, having floral and geometric designs.

In London, Arthur Liberty's products were highly successful in bringing "artistic jewelry" to the public at large. His work combined respect both for the artistic content of a jewel and its commercial appeal. Like Samuel Bing, who opened the commercial gallery Art Nouveau in 1895 in Paris, Arthur Liberty (1845–1917) attained his new style as a result of his fascination with Oriental art.

Foreseeing the innovative potential of industrialization, Liberty agreed to collaborate with industry. This collaboration avoided a conflict between his plan to spread art to the masses and the high cost of handmade objects. Around 1897, new metal products imported from Germany allowed him to produce his own line of jewelry, which he named "Cyrmic." These jewels marked a new direction in both the design and workmanship of personal adornments. They also featured a new style of design for the jewelry of that era: the Celtic revival. Liberty products drew their severe stylization and emphasis on line from this very ancient culture and its jewelry. The work of Archibald Knox (1864–1933) carried Celtic ornamentation to its extremes. He intensified the sense of stylization through his use of rising, curving, and intertwining lines.

At the same time as Liberty House experienced its great success, Theodor Fahrner's firm in Pforzheim, Germany, in operation since the second half of the nineteenth century, established itself

Page from the Calderoni
mail-order sales catalogue,
Milan, 1903.

as the major producer of Jugend-stil decorative objects.

Artistically speaking, Italy at the turn of the century was in a difficult phase, too rooted in classical tradition to be able to create a national style and an artistic language capable of interpreting the great changes of the era. Nineteenth-century eclecticism and the archeological revival of those years still dominated Italian style and design. A lack of creative, innovative imagination was at the root of Italy's relatively late embrace of Art Nouveau compared to other European countries. In fact, the chief purpose of the International Exhibition of Decorative Arts of 1902 in Turin was the consecration of this new art movement in Italy. Meanwhile in the rest of Europe, the movement approached an irreversible crisis.

As elsewhere, the Italian "floral style" is at its best in the fields of applied and decorative arts, producing important contributions in jewelry and metal-working successfully applied to objects for both interior and exterior decoration. Vincenzo Miranda, who was already in business in his shop in Naples by 1899, followed a decidedly modernistic path. His jewelry relied on fine chiseling, plasticity in shape, and small stones. His motifs were also new: women's heads with flowing hair, the play of delicate lines, refined gold flowers on buckles.

The Milanese firm Calderoni also conformed to the new style. Beginning in 1903, the firm included objects inspired by Liberty in its catalogues. The search for a synthesis of functional and artistic values can be seen in these objects. As in other countries, schools like the Umanitaria and the Scuola per Orefici in Milan were established to encourage and train artisans.

In Germany, Pforzheim was a small rural city until 1767 when a few small jewelry and watch manufacturers set up shop there. Later in 1907, Henkel & Grosse established a business that specialized in the production of costume jewelry. During the thirties, the firm worked for Lanvin and Schiaparelli. Since 1955 it has

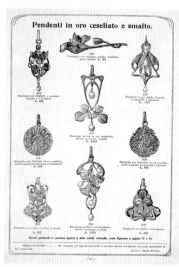

worked exclusively for Dior.

In 1913 Gabrielle Chanel opened her first boutique in Deauville, a seaside resort in France. She herself is a testimonial to the style she endorsed: simple but quietly elegant. Chanel style is characterized by proportion, finishing touches, harmony of color, and the contrast between the humble jersey used to make her dresses and the richness of the real or imitation jewels that she always used to complete every outfit. Chanel has said that it made no difference whether the stones were real or not.

Around 1912 two famous French couturiers, Paul Poiret and Madeleine Vionnet, accessorized their outfits with nonprecious jewelry—true costume jewelry. Poiret used long necklaces with tassels made from silk and semiprecious stones, and the great *parurier* Georges Desrues created great strings of pearls and jewelry for Vionnet's bias-cut dresses. It had finally become possible for a woman to wear nonprecious jewels that had the same characteristics as the real ones. The ivory in Mme. Vionnet's jewelry could be celluloid and the coral nothing more than red-hued stones. Lapis lazuli and amber could be mere imitations. But they were all extremely beautiful and it is beauty that counts in the world of fashion.

A few manufacturers of nonprecious ornaments (Cohn & Rosenberger—then Coro, Trifari, Bliss and Co.—then Napier) had already set out on the road to success in the American market, which was receptive to nonprecious ornaments thanks to the increasing success of the film industry and its silent-film stars that an increasingly wider audience sought to emulate.

Art Deco

These same years saw the beginnings of Art Deco, interrupted by the outbreak of the First World War and therefore belatedly consecrated at the Paris exposition of 1925. At that time, Paris was under the influence of African art as well as Diaghilev's Ballets Russes, with their daring pieces and astonishing sets and costumes. Through the Ballets Russes the rich color contrasts, captured especially by the Fauves, flowed into the aesthetics of jewelry. At no other time has jewelry exhibited such strong chromatic contrasts.

From African art, through the mediation of Cubism and Fauvism, new forms also arose for jewels and nonprecious ornaments, incorporating geometric shape, stylized decoration, and symmetrical line.

In 1919 in Weimar, Germany, Walter Gropius founded the Bauhaus, an arts and crafts institute which found its greatest expression in architecture. Members of the Bauhaus made use of materials never before employed, such as iron, nickel, and chrome, with the intention of reflecting the

An example of "slave"
bracelets, worn by Nancy
Cunard in a photograph by
Man Ray from 1926.

styles of modern life. Thanks to them, design became a form of communicaton and jewelry making became one of its mediums. It was also under the influence of the simple, linear design that took shape in Austria and Germany at that time that jewelry and non-precious ornaments assumed architectural and mechanical forms. By the end of the First World War, Europe's reaction to the horrors and privations was an unbridled show of *joie de vivre*. The so-called Roaring Twenties were notorious for their worship of luxury and novelty. It was a time of avant-garde art movements, of jazz music, of Mistinguett, and Josephine Baker's Revue Nègre.

Paris once again became the cultural reference point for other European countries and for the United States. Paris, in turn, was

strongly influenced by Hollywood movie stars, to whom many women looked for inspiration for a care-free lifestyle. Around this time, hair and fashion accessories were worn more for style than for value and further promoted the emancipated woman, who was finally liberated from the slavery of corsets by Poiret. Short hair, *à la garçonne*, caused combs and hat pins to disappear, replaced by earrings, in particular long hanging ones, intended to enhance the neck. Clips adorned cloche hats and jacket lapels, but also the shoulders and hips in order to show off the female figure. Sautoirs experienced a new burst of popularity. These long necklaces, ending in pendants to emphasize the neckline (and the back), added a touch of femininity to the straight and somewhat severe outfits. Feminine cigarette holders and cases, made of tortoise shell, ebony, and mother-of-pearl, became prized accessories.

In 1922, the discovery of the tomb of King Tutankhamen, which was extremely rich in jewels and decorative objects, unleashed a fashion for Egyptian-inspired jewelry. Elegant women of the time, at ease in their straight flapper dresses and short, geometrical hair styles, showed off long pearl sautoirs, bracelet upon bracelet of Bakelite, worn not only on the wrists but also "slavestyle," on the upper part of the arm, in every style, shape, weight, and color, as

A sautoir worn in back, as seen in a drawing by René Boucher, published in *Vogue*, Paris, 1925.

riencing an economic situation marked by serious inequality and was not able at the time to set aside its national aesthetic and spiritual values in favor of European forms, as its debated participation in the Paris Exposition of 1925 also demonstrated. Taste in Italy in the twenties was therefore contradictory, displaying a revival of the past alongside the newer canons of Futurism. The "aerodynamic" character of the female body was emphasized, following the suggestions of stylists in terms of greater freedom and simplicity in dress. Although pins, clips, jewelry, and necklaces of semiprecious stones were available, the moment for costume jewelry had not yet arrived. It would be long in coming to a society as conservative as Italy at that time. In this regard, the costume jewelry makers of Casalmaggiore, with more than fifty workers in 1906, should be considered an isolated case. The objects they produced, some of them copies, were almost entirely destined for export to the Middle East and to South and Central America. As such, Casalmaggiore is more interesting from an economic viewpoint than from a stylistic one.

Semiprecious and ordinary materials (onyx, lapis lazuli, jade, malachite, coral, ivory, tortoise shell, rhinestones, and marcasite, joined with silver and metal) were, however, abundantly used in the making of accessories such

well as hanging geometrical earrings, and masses of pins. These last were the most representative Deco-style ornament, with their linear, simple shapes symbolizing the modern spirit of the times.

Publications from this period show that Italy in the twenties adapted the French style, following its own particular path defined by the socio-political ferment that consistently marked the opposition between the elevated level of upper-middle-class taste with its elitist products and the mediocre level of the products designed for the public at large. Italy was expe-

as buckles and clasps for hand-bags. These objects are extremely refined and were created by expert craftsmen with the same care given to a precious object.

The White Period and the First Costume Jewels

The Wall Street crash of 1929 caused a serious recession in both America and Europe. The Great Depression of 1930 signaled the decline of Art Deco, which was viewed as antisocial, conservative, and old-fashioned. This consequently also led to a return of the traditional image of femininity: long hair pinned up, ankle-length skirts, and fashions, sometimes historical in nature, with folds and drapes that accentuated the shape of the body and exalted its movements. Large pins for fastening wide hats were back in fashion, as were earrings similar to the platinum and diamond ones worn in France and Spain in the eighteenth century as well as long, hanging ones. Women once again wore clips and simple pearl necklaces or elaborate ones with large stones. In fact, clips worn at the neckline, on the lapel, and also at the waist and in the hair were prominent emblems of the decade.

With the disappearance of their gilded-age clients, many jewelers turned to the manufacture of nonprecious objects more in keeping with an era of reduced means. Thus, the costume jewelry industry blossomed, freed from the classical traditions of precious jewelry.

Meanwhile, in Pforzheim at the beginning of the 1930s, designers were experimenting with a new mold-casting technique—centrifugal casting, imported from Sweden. The innovative aspect of this system consisted in forcing the liquid substances to adhere to the sides of a mold through the strong pressure exerted by the high rotary speed of the centrifuge. Objects made this way are defined, precise, and identical to the original model, requiring no additional welding or finishing touches. Centrifugal casting, primarily applied to metals in Pforzheim, broadened the horizons of the costume jewelry industry. This new technique allowed the industry to greatly expand the possible range of patterns and to streamline work procedures, resulting in remarkable cost savings. In 1932, again in Pforzheim, clear nickel-plating was perfected. This method of hot-polishing white metals is much faster and more efficient than the older cold-nickel technique that resulted in an opaque finish. Hot-nickel plating requires no additional hand finishing.

In Providence, Rhode Island, the most important manufacturers of costume jewelry soon adopted the innovations developed in Pforzheim. Beginning in 1938, these manufacturers also fine-tuned techniques for gilding and

Page from a catalogue
issued by the Società
Federale Orefici of
Casalmaggiore, c. 1910.

soon marketed objects in an extraordinary variety of themes and subjects. During these same years, thanks to the reforms enacted by Roosevelt's New Deal, America began to recover from the Great Depression that followed the 1929 Crash. A wave of optimism swept the country and encouraged a break with the past and its traditions. Showy, exuberant designs replaced the elegant, straight, moderate designs of the twenties. The new style, typified by Hollywood stars, featured enormous stones, some cabochon-cut and set in manufactured mounts.

Plastics also enjoyed great success because they were well suited to mechanized manufacturing processes. Without a great deal of difficulty, they could be molded, carved, and dyed to yield the geometric shapes popular in those days.

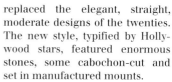

The pliability of synthetic materials led to the creation of a modernistic style in necklaces and bracelets featuring linked, geometric pieces of colored plastic and chrome-plated metal strung on elastic. Firms such as Henkel & Grosse and Jacob Bengel, in Pforzheim, and others in Oynnax in the French Jura specialized in this type of jewelry, which was also popular elsewhere in Europe. The Auguste Bonaz firm was the preeminent manufacturer of this style of jewelry in the Jura.

In 1934 in a book dedicated to the art of fine jewelry and

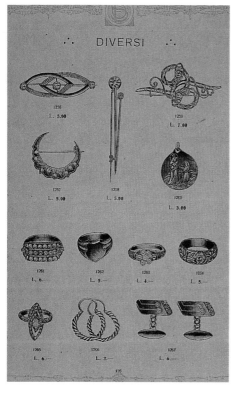

Jakob Bengel necklace,
Idar Oberstein, Germany,
c. 1930. Handworked
galalith and chrome.

costume jewelry, Paul Poiret, a member of one of the most famous French metalworking firms, decreed the death of jewels that were mere copies of real ones and the birth of a completely autonomous genre: "Costume jewelry, bound in the past to the copying of real jewels and therefore called 'imitation jewelry,' has now freed itself from the slavery of copying and now produces moderate-priced ornaments with complete autonomy."

By this time, the prevailing taste in jewelry, in contrast to the recent past with its excesses and bright, contrasting colors, imposed a generally white palette. The color white was enshrined at an exhibit at the Palais Galleria in Paris in 1929. This tendency extended both to fashion—where white satin and gauze took the honors—and to precious and costume jewelry.

Maison Burma in France interpreted "white" to the letter. Beginning in 1929, Burma introduced faithful reproductions of jewels made from silver and Swarovski crystal stones—perfect and handmade—to the French national market. Burma's fame spread to America, thanks also to a clever publicity campaign that used famous personalities from the theater and art worlds as modern tes-

timonials to the phenomenon. In 1930, the Union of Costume Jewelry Manufacturers opened its first exhibition in Paris at the Hôtel Moderne. Thus, costume jewelry set off on the road to the world of fashion, a road which ran from France to America and back again. Costume jewelry spread from country to country, its form and traits slightly altered in each nation.

In Paris in 1937, Elsa Schiaparelli presented her famous collection of outfits inspired by circus themes, accessorized with metal jewelry designed by Jean Schlumberger. Schiaparelli's favored designs—fanciful, simple and cheerful, new and witty, inspired by Surrealism and Dadaism—were widely taken up by American magazines. Even more so than in the past, American manufacturers abandoned customary jewelry themes and created playful objects, displaying an easy style in perfect harmony with their way of life.

During the years 1920 to 1930, Italy was characterized by the gradual encroachment of Fascist ideology on the arts. The Fascists controlled a tight network of associations, networks, and academies in an attempt to subjugate art as an instrument of national affairs. Fascist art was expected to be simultaneously traditional and

Diana Vreeland, the legendary editor of American *Vogue*.

modern. It was supposed to honor the Roman tradition and also perform its propagandistic duties. This was especially true of painting, sculpture, and architecture.

However, painting and sculpture, as well as film making and literature, did not endorse the predominant Fascist themes; among them the idea of a woman as wife, mother, and homemaker. Craftsmen, however, working in the applied arts, had a greater measure of freedom. In fact, the decorative arts tended to address themselves to upper-middle-class society whose *femmes fatales* were perennially chattering on their lily-white telephones.

Fine jewelry making offered geometrical styles that existed side by side with naturalistic themes, especially toward the end of the decade. Tortoise shell, mother-of-pearl, and coral in a variety of colors, cut into beads, small canes, and drops, were widely used. At the time, these materials were still considered affordable and could be sold at prices that made them available to a large part of the population.

Synthetic stones were used to imitate the "white" style then popular in neighboring France. By 1936 clips, brooches, and buckles became rounder. A bracelet made by Alfredo Ravasco, a remarkable individual in the world of Italian jewelry making of the period, is a splendid example of the "white

period." Exhibited at the Fifth Milan Triennial, this bracelet, executed in platinum and diamond, is so sumptuous in its symmetrical curving motifs that it resembles a band of lace.

In 1936–1937 Italy established a policy of economic self-sufficiency, and so began to market a national fashion, which up until then, thanks to the exchange of ideas provided by the large international shows in Milan, Venice, and Rome, had not permitted stereotyped production.

In 1935 France witnessed a turnabout in style that was in perfect accord with developments in painting. The geometric motifs that represented the typical Art Deco style were transformed into curving shapes, giving rise to arabesques that often evoked nature. Necklaces made with "gas-tube" and "rat-tail" chains came into fashion. Diana Vreeland, the legendary editor of American *Vogue*, popularized Cartier's "Moor's head" brooches.

Official recognition of these trends took place at the Paris Exhibition of 1937, which was attended by both fine jewelry and costume jewelry makers. It was the last opportunity for such a gathering before the outbreak of the Second World War.

The Hollywood Years

Beginning in 1936, in order to avoid persecution by the Nazis, many Jewish goldsmiths and jewelers emigrated from Europe to the United States. Many of them turned to the manufacturing of costume ornaments, a rapidly expanding field that was open to new ideas and technical innovation.

Those who left Europe were not allowed to take precious metals or money with them. But many managed to smuggle out rhinestones and imitation stones, which were also banned for export by the Nazis. On the one hand, this prohibition required American manufacturers of costume jewelry to resort to indigenous materials (plastic in all its varieties, turquoise, mother-of-pearl, coral,

shells) or to enamels in order to simulate colored stones. On the other hand, some manufacturers made use of the considerable amount of imitation stones smuggled into this country by the exiles.

As a result, American costume jewelry of the early forties was either gold or made with stones. Gold lent itself to being "colored" through the use of different alloys and took on unexpected nuances, from pink, to green, to blue. Gold was also paired with turquoise, coral, and rock crystal, given the difficulty in finding precious gems (platinum and all the white metals were rationed because of the war), or it was accompanied by a large amount of colored stones. Among these, imitation topaz was preeminent, made popular by the Duchess of Windsor, who was especially fond of topaz. Additionally, some of the stones brought over from Europe were used to make large chunky bracelets, shiny in their whiteness, or highly colored like Indian bracelets, which were perfect for an evening getaway.

The decade from 1940 to 1950 witnessed the growing supremacy of American culture over European culture. New York became the world art capital and Hollywood and its stars defined the international style of the moment. Marlene Dietrich, Greta Garbo, and Joan Crawford were the idols of the time, and the American woman emulated their attitudes,

Marlene Dietrich, one of the most famous movie stars, was the ideal model for women in the Hollywood Years.

as well as their dresses and accessories. For the first time, fashion was conceived and carried out with the American sporty, easygoing lifestyle in mind, rather than drawing on French *haute couture*, an expression of elegance dating back to bourgeois traditions and designed for the well-bred woman.

The ornaments produced in this period became indispensable for updating the short, simple dresses that had been designed to save on fabric, which had been rationed because of the war. Patriotic pins (flags, wings, anchors) symbolized a solidarity with the men engaged overseas; flowers, hearts, and animal pins expressed sentimental and natural themes.

After the War: The Supremacy of Paris

As the anguish and deprivations of the war began to subside, the world of fashion timidly raised its head. Slowly at first, but later with increasing determination and purpose, people turned back to the pleasures of fashion. The fashion industry also served as a source of jobs and possible wealth.

In 1947 Dior launched his New Look collection in Paris and revived the image of the feminine, romantic woman. Rounded shoulders replaced padded ones, waist-

Group of patriotic pins.
Trifari, United States, early
1940s. Stamped Trifari.
Gold-plated silver and
rhinestones.

lines were tight, and skirts rose to calf length. The bust was emphasized and necklines plunged, sometimes giddily.

The fashion magazines of the time were quick to pick up on the rush of events that once again brought Paris to the forefront of world fashion. The December issue of *Vogue* featured photographs and descriptions of an incredible number of fashion accessories, especially nonprecious ornaments and jewelry. These items were produced by individuals who were to become the most famous designers in their field in the ensuing decades. Costume jewelry coexisted with real jewels, sometimes on the same outfit and sometimes even in the same piece of jewelry. In America, postwar prosperity and the optimism which naturally resurfaces at the end of a major calamity created an atmosphere conducive to fashion. The shapes of costume jewelry became increasingly like those of real jewels. The majority of designers preferred traditional jewelry styles. Schlumberger and Verdura, however, drew their themes from nature, mythology, and art history. Both designers reached the height of their success around the mid-sixties.

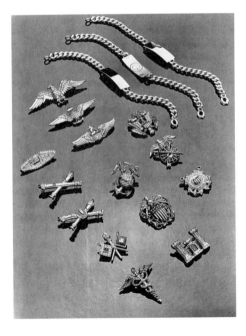

The predominant color for both costume and real jewelry in the fifties seems to have been white, and later on turquoise. The influence of the New Look in America, and the American designers' liberal interpretation of this look, resulted in rather showy jewelry: large brooches accentuating the bust and long earrings framing the face. Exaggerated gems, like the ones sold by Indian Maharajas, adorned complicated upswept hairdos.

Christian Dior's "coral line" in a drawing by Christian Bérard, published in *Vogue*.

At her husband's inaugural ball in 1952, Mamie Eisenhower wore an imitation pearl and rhinestone parure created especially for her by Trifari, America's most well-known costume jewelry maker. Marilyn Monroe incarnated the ambiguous nature of the relationship between real and fake jewelry as she sang "Diamonds Are a Girl's Best Friend" while wearing a rhinestone and rhodium-plated parure. These jewels accentuated her exuberant blonde beauty, and nobody missed the diamonds.

The only exceptions to the return to tradition were Rebayes's copper and silver jewelry and Renoir's copper and occasionally enameled pieces. These jewels were designed for a young, educated, and carefree audience.

Unlike in America, where costume jewelry designers generally imitated real jewels, French high-fashion jewelry designers took a different tack. In fact, French couturiers scorned imitation jewels and focused instead on creating *bijoux de couture*. According to the French, couture jewelry should be special and change with fashion. In essence, a piece of jewelry should be a way of individualizing an outfit and accentuating its color and fabric.

Ornaments produced in limited runs for French haute couture were often a source of inspiration for the costume jewelry designed for a broader public. In America, fashion jewelry was sold in luxury department stores where an ever-increasing amount of floor space was reserved for this type of jewelry.

Even though French couturiers received all the credit for having launched the vogue for *bijoux de couture*, and indirectly for costume jewelry, other sectors of the fashion industry played important supporting roles. Designers, manufacturers, and distributors made decisive contributions to the success of costume jewelry. The names of many of these individuals and corporations still go unrecognized today. Among them are Max Boinet, Robert Goossens, Maison Gripoix, G. Desrues, Rousselet, C.I.S., Scemama, Rose Idée, Francis Winter, Roger Jean-Pierre, Lola

Drawing by Emilio Pucci of
a piece of jewelry produced
by Coppola & Toppo, early
1960s. Private collection.

Prusac, Maryse Blanchard, Jeanne Péral, Monique Vedié, Madeleine Rivière, Renel, René Llonguet, and Simone Dumas.

Having regained her femininity, the New Look woman wanted refined, classic, sumptuous jewelry: rivières festooned with drop crystals, *colliers de chien,* cameo brooches in an antique style that complemented the new, gracefully retrospective silhouette. Styles from the past came back into fashion—from the garland style to the Victorian, neoclassical, and romantic. This last was magnificently reinterpreted by Francis Winter.

Christian Dior, a man who loved tradition, was the first to intuit the potential innovative power of the new type of crystal stones perfected by Swarowski. Dior christened these stones "Aurora Borealis" because of their iridescent colors obtained through a new vaporizing technique. *Bijoux de couture* created from these stones possessed unprecedented uniqueness and innovative beauty.

Stepping back onto the stage of international fashion, Chanel reopened her fashion house in 1954. She resurrected her classic suit, combining it with clusters of gold-plated, imitation pearl and colored-crystal sautoirs, glass-paste Byzantine necklaces, and button earrings with a pearl in the center.

In Italy the effects of the war, as well as the government's policy of economic self-sufficiency and prohibition on imports of foreign materials and models, forced jewelry designers to be independent. They had to exploit their creativity to the fullest and draw inspiration from materials at hand, such as coral from Naples and Torre del Greco, Venetian glass, cork, shells, and raffia and wool to make tassels.

During the war, everything was done in an effort to stay in business. It was symptomatic of the times that an established firm like Calderoni in Milan abandoned the field of fine jewelry, and turned to the manufacture of metal trinkets. These products were distributed by Gi. Vi. Emme, a manufacturer of perfumes and cosmetics that had likewise abandoned its original field for lack of materials. Their collaboration lasted until 1946, offering opportunities for work for two firms which would otherwise have been in a state of serious crisis. Incredibly, even during the war, the manufacture and sale of fashion trimmings continued. They were made of bone, feathers, metal, and galalith and were often finished with enamel to make up for the lack of stones.

The firms most often cited in the fashion magazines that continued to publish at the time were Ceriano and Riesla in Milan, Alba in Genoa, Gingillo, Cavestri, Alda, as well as Fratti, also in Milan, and finally Luciana in Rome. At the end of the war and throughout the fifties, certain names recur: Artea, specializing in varnished terracotta jewelry with archaic classical themes, and Ottavio Re, both from Milan; Carlo Deagostini from Turin, for his imitation jewels; A.N.M.A. and Myricae of Rome, which made its name in 1949 with a collection of classical jewelry.

The first exports of costume jewelry to France (Coppola & Toppo for Schiaparelli, Jacques Fath, Piguet, and Molyneux in 1949) and to America (Fratta at the beginning of the forties, and Emma Caini Pellini in the early fifties) signaled the rise of costume jewelry making in Italy. The industry became a reality in Florence in 1951 with the inauguration of the "Made in Italy" style, at the hands of Gian Battista Giorgioni.

In the beginning, costume jewelry was generally made by artisans. (Among the few exceptions to this practice was Calestani of Milan, originally from Casalmaggiore.) Production was often managed by families or, occassionally, by small firms. Their products were valuable, but lacked the durability and stable properties typical of industrially produced costume jewelry.

Furthermore, the attitude of the Italian public did not help foster a rapid increase in the use of costume jewelry as a complement to an outfit. Throughout the fifties, costume jewelry was viewed as an unseemly substitute for the real thing. Souvenir jewelry made of local materials (coral in Naples and Torre del Greco; glass in Venice; mosaic, braided silk, burnished silver and metal in Florence), following traditional techniques, continued to sell. But costume jewelry, which in any case had to blend appropriately with the family jewels, still struggled to establish itself.

Trinkets fashioned from imitation pearls and rhinestones, in traditional shapes taken from French jewelry, were the most common. The most well-known Italian "replicator" of French jewelry is Giuliano Fratti, who was already famous by the beginning of the forties. A man of great insight, Fratti is capable of reinventing a wide variety of styles, designs, and materials

Sketch of an earring for
Coppola & Toppo, Mila
Schön, 1967.

from countries and traditions foreign to Italians and adapting them to suit Italian taste. A few years later, Canalesi of Milan, Cascio and Bijoux Sandra, both of Florence, also appeared on the scene as "interpreters" of French-style jewelry. During the fifties, very few Italian creators attempted to exploit traditional local materials to their best advantage. Most jewelry makers remained faithful to the stylistic conventions of French jewelry.

Foremost among the jewelers who distanced themselves from the French tradition is Coppola & Toppo, the most widely known Italian firm abroad. Coppola & Toppo is famous for its whimsical creations using crystal stones in matching colors, set in free and easy shapes. Their products were designed for export to the French and American markets.

Two other firms, Emma Caimi Pellini and Ornella, dedicated themselves to the production of costume jewelry made from typically Italian materials (Venetian glass, raffia, ceramics, and plastics), using shapes and subjects linked to Italian culture.

With their rich, highly crafted products, Borbonese in Turin and Elfe in Florence staked out their territory at a point midway between imitation and costume jewelry.

In 1956 the Centro Romano per l'Alta Moda Italiana was founded in Rome. Meanwhile, costume jewelry moved from continent to continent: Italians exported to America, and Napier, one of the most important American manufacturers, was chosen by Sorelle Fontana to accessorize their collection.

The Triumph of "Made in Italy"

As the sixites rolled on, high fashion lost ground to a total liberation in dress and behavior, inspired and defined by the youth generation. Young people no longer felt defined by a specific national culture; what they did feel was an irresistible desire for something new.

Paco Rabanne's metallic knit outfits, which looked as if an entire dress had been turned into a piece of jewelry, and Courrège's clingy, white, space-age dresses paired with helmets and large

Dress by Ognibene-Zendaman, c. 1965. A shower of multicolored organdy flowers on this transparent plastic gown creates a new space-age romanticism.

white sunglasses were both inspired by contemporary abstract art. But these designs and the collections of Yves Saint-Laurent, Givenchy, Pierre Cardin, Ungaro, and Lanvin, all of which were finished with jewelry specially attuned to their outfits, had little influence on fashion in the streets.

There, everything was accepted and people could choose their own mode of dress. Yesterday's creations were no longer relegated to the past, but took on a new life. This anarchy in dress coincided with a new way of looking at

life and its problems. Fashion became a product for the masses, very far removed from the elitist models of haute couture.

Young hippies placed new value on ethnic jewelry, exotic and intense colors, bright-colored fabrics, and ornaments, many made from recycled materials such as cans, silverware, even tires.

The cool, geometric lines of haute couture outfits remained the prerequisite of the upper class. Young people preferred soft, casual shapes: outfits inspired by Indian costumes, Mary Quant's miniskirts, and short leather jackets and blue jeans like those worn by Marlon Brando in *On the Waterfront*.

At the beginning of the sixties, a variety of factors contributed to a change in the nature of costume jewelry in Italy. Rome took over Hollywood's position as the capital of the international film world. An obligatory stop for any star who wanted to be seen, Rome was like a shop window where one could gaze upon the lives and loves of celebrities. Elizabeth Taylor and Richard Burton fell in love in 1963 on the set of *Cleopatra* and their story spread around the world. The historical style developed for the film set the trend for current fashion: dramatic make-up, elaborate hairdos, bright colors, and opulent jewelry.

The rich variety of products and styles of workmanship available in "Made in Italy" lines dur-

Group of jewels, Line
Vautrin, c. 1950. Silver-
plated and partially
enameled bronze. Private
collection, New York.

ing those years was highly valued.
The prestige of Italian products
was so great that in 1960, Nieman
Marcus, the owner of the chain of
department stores of the same
name, organized a huge party to
honor a delegation of Italian tailors, artisans, diplomats, journal-
ists, and photographers.

Meanwhile, French high fashion changed the very nature of the
bijou de couture, treating it as an intrinsic part of an outfit and not
merely as a simple accessory. Designers chose jewelry that emphasized the colors, shapes, or ideas
linked to the themes of a collection.
In Italy, where the fashion trends
in neighboring France were always
of great interest, some
manufacturers fol-
lowed the same path,
dedicating themselves
to making more target-
ed ornaments than in
the past. Others con-
centrated on making
the most of Italian tra-
ditions and materials;
for example, Lisa di
Firenze or Luciana de
Reutern, who reinter-
preted Etruscan and
Roman jewelry.

Within a few years,
in both Milan and
Rome (Venice, alas,
continued to be con-
strained by outmoded,
stale styles) jewelry de-
signers learned to in-

terpret the international vogue for
costume jewelry in their own fashion and in a language all their own.

The coexistence of different
styles, enlivened by the recently
introduced prêt-à-porter collections, resulted in luxurious and
opulent fashions in which historical and ethnic references were
blended with neo-baroque forms.
For jewelry, the best interpreters
of this emphatic style were Bozart
for Tita Rossi and Borbonese for
Valentino in Italy, and Kenneth
Jay Lane in the United States.

Beginning in the mid-sixties,
Lane was able to convince the
international jet set to accept
costume jewelry. With great intel-

Headgear and vest. Created
by Paolo Scheggi for
Germana Marucelli.
Worn by Franca Scheggi
Dall'Acqua.

ligence and a sense of irony, he
put forward replicas of opulent
jewels from great firms such as
Webb, Cartier, Bulgari, and Harry
Winston.

At the same time, the hippie
movement encouraged the creation of vividly colored pseudo-
ethnic ornaments to be worn on
loud, contrasting patterned fabrics. Other influences took jewelry
design in different directions. London's Mod movement, which up-
held a certain formal elegance in
dress, and Paco Rabanne's oufits
made of metallic sheets, which
drew on the avant-garde op and
pop art movements, created a desire for jewelry and nonprecious
ornaments in pure, abstract
shapes. This jewelry was often
fashioned in metal and plastic.

Germana Maruccelli, an artist
and tailor in Milan, deserves
greater recognition than she currently enjoys. As long ago as the
early sixties, she gathered together
a group of artists (Fontana, Crippa,
Arnaldo Pomodoro, Alviani, Gentili, and Scheggi) to create the trinkets and jewels that she wanted for
her outfits. Today, the "artists' jewels" created for her are a perfect
illustration of the "pure" and "spa-
tial" ornaments of the sixties. Although originating from formal research with a shorter tradition, the
spatial-style ornaments made by
Merù in Milan, Cascio, Fiuschi,
and Elfe in Florence, as well as the
inlaid-wood ornaments by Diana

Monili of Milan are nevertheless
quite striking.

Both in the United States and
in Europe, some makers of costume jewelry took yet another
path and followed the trends of
fine jewelry inspired by abstract
expressionism and action painting. The structure of this jewelry
is disjointed and its appearance
often verges on the grotesque.

Beginning in the middle of the
sixties, in a protectionist effort to
stem the tide of Italian costume
jewelry, America increased its import taxes so that the original
price of any item was quadrupled.
This did not, however, stop Italian
products from continuing to meet
with widespread approval.

BROOCHES IN ARCHITECTURAL SHAPES

Manufacturer
Vase of flowers:
unidentified
Mosque and pagoda:
unknown

Place and Date of Manufacture
France, early 1900s

Materials and Techniques
Silver fretwork (vase of flowers, mosque); cast silver and rhinestones (pagoda)

Mark
Paris silver mark and illegible manufacturer's mark (vase of flowers); Paris silver mark (mosque)

Provenance
Private collection, Milan

Jewels and semiprecious ornaments in the Edwardian style are important because for the first time these objects were conceived as accessories for the fashions of the era, which tended to be light though sumptuous. Therefore, the jewelry is small, delicately made, in white or clear stones with a touch of color.

The pieces reproduced here exemplify this style, both in their classical subject matter and in the way they were made—some by hand, others worked entirely by machine.

The rhinestone-covered silver mosque-shaped brooch (at left) and the vase of flowers (above right) are of handworked fretwork. The vase rests on a base of four horizontally set rhinestone baguettes. The main portal of the mosque is set off by a rhinestone baguette on either side of the entryway, while four carré-cut green rhinestones rest like a necklace at the base of the cupola. The pagoda brooch (above left) is of cast pavé-set rhinestones.

BROOCH IN THE SHAPE OF AN OWL'S HEAD

The owl is one of the most frequently recurring motifs in the jewelry of the late nineteenth and early twentieth centuries. In traditional folklore, the owl is associated with misfortune and death. But when worn as a talisman, this bird assures success in all efforts requiring preparation and skill. The rhinestones in this brooch are in a closed setting, forming a double rounded framework. The outer framework defines the shape of the owl's head, while the inner one outlines the eyes. The eyes themselves are made of two large, faceted, pink oval stones, surrounded by a ring of rhinestones, also set "a notte." On the back, a bar connects the outermost sides of the larger framework. The two settings that form the eyes are fastened to the bar with two hand-fixed rivets. As the base is made of metal, there are no punches and it is therefore impossible to determine either the jewel's exact provenance or the name of the maker. However, the quality of the stones and the handworking (stonecutting, mounting, riveting, and openwork) lead one to believe that this is a very high-quality piece of jewelry, such as those that were usually made in the best Parisian workshops.

Place and Date of Manufacture
England or France, early 1900s

Materials and Techniques
Cast metal, rhinestones

Mark
None

Provenance
Terzo Millennio Collection, Milan

BROOCHES IN THE SHAPE OF ANIMALS

Manufacturer
Lizard: unidentified

Place and Date of Manufacture
Monkey: Germany
Insect: France or England
Lizard: Austria or Germany, early 1900s

Materials and Techniques
Monkey and lizard: cast silver, rhinestones
Insect: cast metal, rhinestones

Mark
Monkey: Sterling Germany
Insect: none
Lizard: 935 (maker illegible)

Provenance
Private collection, Milan

Animals are a favorite motif for jewelry and nonprecious ornaments, in part because different animals symbolize human traits and features. For example, in all cultures the lizard is linked to eyesight, and it is said that it can protect the eyes because of its green, emerald-like color.

In the monkey brooch, the animal is profiled picking up a ball made of a cabochon onyx stone. Châton-cut, pavé-set rhinestones form the body, and a green rhinestone marks the eye.

The insect (below left) is made of châton-cut, pavé-set rhinestones spaced with faceted green and red glass stones. Five red rhinestones of descending size separate the two wings and two more red rhinestones form the eyes. Five green rhinestones delineate the head.

The lizard brooch was cast in silver; the body is composed of clear rhinestones, with a rivière of green rhinestones running down the center.

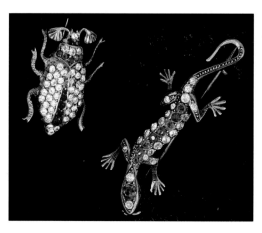

DROP EARRINGS

Place and Date of Manufacture
England or France, early 1900s

Materials and Techniques
Open-work silver, colorless rhinestones

Mark
None

Provenance
Costanza Fiani Collection, Milan

Without a doubt, the forget-me-not is the most common floral motif of the Victorian Age because of the romantic meaning of the flower's name. In an era when the sentimental connotations of jewelry were of overriding importance, wearing a forget-me-not symbolized the steadfastness of love. Just as a flower drops its petals once it is cut, the wearer would die of pain if abandoned by her partner. Thousands of examples of this motif exist both in jewelry and on fabrics, in enamelware and niello, as if the simplicity and loveliness of this shape, coupled with the romance of the flower's name, made it especially pleasing to anyone who saw it.

The earrings are of open-work silver with châton-cut rhinestones. The upper part consists of a rose-shaped cluster of seven rhinestones, resting on a leafy support. The pendant is a wreathlike volute encircling the forget-me-not; a single, larger, châton-cut rhinestone forms the pistil. These earrings are jewels of refined elegance and delicate workmanship.

BROOCH WITH AMPHORA

**Place and Date
of Manufacture**
England or the United
States, early 1900s

**Materials and
Techniques**
Die-cast brass, trimmed
by hand and treated

Mark
None

Provenance
Antichità De Giovanni
Collection, Milan

The Arts & Crafts movement revisited and re-worked classical motifs, sometimes in an overly simplified fashion. When this excessive simplification did not occur, as is the case with a few pieces of jewelry from that era that have survived, we can refer to such jewels as true art objects, with all that the term implies, including market value.

The brooch pictured on this page, however, is intended to be an example of a "humble" ornament, without any artistic aspirations. It exemplifies the type of object that was produced by machine in its initial stage and then finished by hand. The creator of the piece hoped to demonstrate the aesthetic superiority of handworked objects over those mass-produced by machines.

In this brooch the amphora was produced by die casting. The sheet of brass that constitutes the base was treated with acids to enliven the surface and oxidized to obtain the green highlights.

OVAL BROOCH WITH SIMULATED AMETHYSTS

This brooch, produced by the Arts & Crafts movement, illustrates the kind of humble ornament that consciously adopted the decorative style and subjects of antiquity, in this case the Greek fret motif.

Italians think of the amethyst as a sad stone because its color evokes death and mourning. But this stone is very popular in Anglo-Saxon countries, where violet is seen as a symbol of royalty and the monarchy. Here, four transparent, faceted, crystal stones are asymmetrically placed, adding brilliance to the center of the piece.

The brooch was made from two sheets of copper. The sheet used for the outline, engraved with the Greek fret motif, is soldered to the central plate. This second sheet, treated with acids in order to create a rough, animated surface, is carved with curling motifs in relief, forming the letter "M."

Place and Date
of Manufacture
England or the United
States, early 1900s

Materials and
Techniques
Copper plate cut, bent
by hand, engraved,
and treated with
acid; faceted stones
simulating amethysts

Mark
None

Provenance
Antichità De Giovanni
Collection, Milan

FLOWER BROOCH

Place and Date of Manufacture
United States, early 1900s

Materials and Techniques
Handworked and hand-embossed sheet of silver and coral

Mark
Hand Made M. J. M. Sterling

Provenance
Private collection, Milan

The choice of a flower as a decorative device is perfectly consistent with Arts & Crafts and Art Nouveau naturalism, both of which moved away from the realistic interpretation of nature typical of the nineteenth century. Arts & Crafts and Art Nouveau designers, influenced by Japanese art, preferred a poetic, almost painterly, transformation of nature both in their choice of colors and their approach to stylization.

Delicately modeled, this brooch depicts a flower just beginning to open on a leafy base. The pistil consists of a red coral drop. The stem, with its sinuous line, is embellished with three finely hammered leaves with defined veining. Since the maker's initials and the inscription "Hand Made" were engraved by hand rather than stamped with a punch, it is logical to assume that very few copies of this object were produced. It is probably the work of an artisan who had not registered a trademark under his name.

HAND MADE
M.J.M.

METAL AND GLASS NECKLACE

This necklace is an example of how the American costume jewelry industry, since its origin, has been able to adopt cultural trends from other countries to suit its own resources. In accordance with the English Arts & Crafts movement, this ornament was probably originally handmade; in the United States, however, it was mass-produced, created with skill and taste, and destined for a wide audience. The necklace is silver-plated metal with ribbed oval and bell-shaped links, alternating with colored glass-paste beads, some are fluted, others faceted or smooth. The spheres are arranged in a precise chromatic progresion, in shades of azure, blue, green, and iron-red, imitating respectively turquoise, lapis lazuli, amazonite, agate, and carnelian stones. An incised triangular-shaped pendant attaches to three glass-and-metal links and red glass-paste beads.

The necklace was shown at the "All That Glitters" exhibit, held at the Bass Museum of Art in Miami from December 18, 1994 to February 2, 1995.

Place and Date of Manufacture
The United States, early 1900s

Materials and Techniques
Silver-plated stamped metal, multicolored glass-paste beads

Mark
None

Provenance
Terzo Millenio Collection, Milan

BUCKLE WITH HERONS

Manufacturer
Piel Frères

**Place and Date
of Manufacture**
France, early 1900s

**Materials and
Techniques**
Cast metal, cloisonné
enameling, glass paste

Mark
P. F.

Provenance
Robin Feldman
Collection, New York

Rendered in brilliant colors, this buckle illustrates the fluid elegance of Art Nouveau, which frequently borrowed motifs from Japanese art.

The piece consists of two nearly identical buckles cast in gold-plated metal depicting a pair of herons seen in profile. The wings of the birds are spread and turned outward. Enamelwork in blue and green tones, in alternating chromatic shades, defines their plumage. An irregular oval of sky-blue glass paste separates the two herons. Their feet rest on a cabochon of turquoise glass paste. One half of the buckle has a second, larger round cabochon, also made of turquoise glass paste. This stone is supported by the beaks and wings of the herons. This decorative element, constituting the buckle's juncture, links the two parts of the ornament and gives the whole a harmonious symmetry.

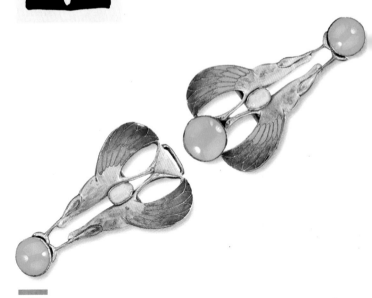

PEACOCK FEATHER BUCKLE AND BUTTONS

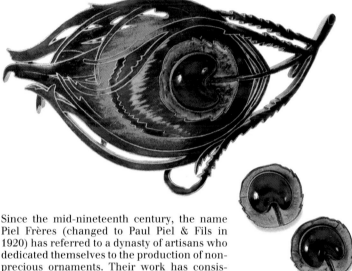

Since the mid-nineteenth century, the name Piel Frères (changed to Paul Piel & Fils in 1920) has referred to a dynasty of artisans who dedicated themselves to the production of non-precious ornaments. Their work has consistently displayed the sort of aesthetic and artistic research worthy of the finest jewelry.

When the Chambre Syndicale de la Bijouterie de Fantasie was founded in Paris in 1873, Alexander Piel became president of the organization. The post then passed to his son Léon Paul Piel, who received the Grand Prix at the Paris exposition in 1900. Léon Paul was also awarded a prize at the St. Louis World's Fair in 1904.

This buckle, published in the *Revue de la Bijouterie* in 1901, depicts a typical Art Nouveau subject, the peacock feather, beloved by artists for its elegant, sinuous patterns and contours. Here it is executed in polychrome enamel in blue, reddish brown, dark green, and in the center, light green tones trimmed in gold plate. A cobalt-blue glass-paste stone, in the shape of a bean, is set in the middle of the pin. The two graceful round buttons repeat the design.

Manufacturer
Piel Frères

Place and Date of Manufacture
France, early 1900s

Materials and Techniques
Gold plate and cloisonné enameled metal in dark colors, glass paste

Mark
P. F.

Provenance
Robin Feldman Collection, New York

STYLIZED BUTTERFLY NECKLACE

Designer
Georges Pierre

Manufacturer
Georges Pierre

Place and Date of Manufacture
France, 1900–1905

Materials and Techniques
Engraved horn and silk ribbon

Mark
GIP

Provenance
Marie José Barillet Collection, Milan

Georges Pierre is one of the best-known creators of jewelry made from horn. The horn is hand polished until it is rendered into thin sheets which are then engraved and inlaid. Pierre's pieces can generally be identified because almost all of them bear the engraved signature G. I. P. At first, Pierre was a competitor of Elizabeth Bonté, a creator of similar jewelry, but he later went into partnership with her. They worked together in French Jura until the mid-1930s. Also from the same period and similar in form to the horn jewelry are the stamped glass-paste jewels created in France by Lalique, Daum, Argy-Rousseau, and Almeric Walter. Today their creations meet the standards of true works of art because of the high artistic level of their design and craftsmanship.

This necklace is made of a brown silk ribbon attached to small gold-plated links and the engraved horn pendant. The stylized butterfly pendant supports a hanging drop.

NECKLACE WITH BUTTERFLY PENDANT

Designer
Elisabeth Bonté

Manufacturer
Elisabeth Bonté

Place and Date of Manufacture
France, early 1900s

Materials and Techniques
Engraved and painted horn, glass paste, carnelian, fine silk cord

Mark
E. Bonté

Provenance
Private collection, Milan

The French-born Elisabeth Bonté is another well-known designer of horn jewelry. Her jewelry is identifiable by the signature that appears on all of her products, with the exception of a few very fragile ones whose durability would be compromised by engraving. Her classic sautoirs with pendants shaped like dragonflies, butterflies, or exotic flowers and finished with an oblong drop stone are well known. A few of her lockets are also quite famous. The lockets depict completely original themes such as a very beautiful winter landscape in which, against a background blanketed by snow, the outline of a pearl-colored tree stands out, its color echoing that of the ice. The necklace shown here consists of a double strand of dark brown silk, interspersed with blue glass-paste spheres with earth-colored inclusions imitating turquoise, and carnelian ovals (the stones can be seen in the smaller photograph). The butterfly pendant, with its outspread wings, is engraved horn painted with a thin layer of pearly enamel. The body is an oval glass-paste cabochon stone which supports a second drop-shaped stone, both of them simulating turquoise.

NECKLACE WITH BELLFLOWER PENDANT

Place and Date of Manufacture
France, early 1900s

Materials and Techniques
Engraved horn, amber ovals, thin silk cord

Mark
None

Provenance
Carolle Thibaut-Pomerantz Collection, Paris

In recent years the use of ivory and horn, like that used to create the pendant for this necklace, has been prohibited in an effort to save endangered species. Previously, large quantities of horn were used to make combs, especially in the second half of the nineteenth century when the price of tortoise shell became too high for most consumers. After being cut into sections, horn was softened in salted boiling water and then either pressed or molded between heated dies or engraved and carved by hand. For Art Nouveau pieces, horn was bleached with a chemical solution containing lead monoxide and soda.

The necklace reproduced here has a thin brown silk cord interspersed with amber oval beads. The pendant depicts a bellflower with five petals and two small leaves emerging from a long shoot, all made from bleached horn. The pendant rests inside a circular, naturalistic frame, also in horn, but darker in color because the horn was not treated.

HINGED BRACELET

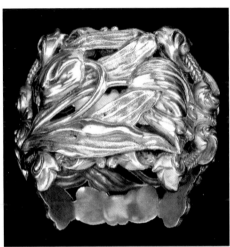

Place and Date of Manufacture
Probably France,
early 1900s

Materials and Techniques
Silver-plated stamped
metal

Mark
None

Provenance
Antichità De Giovanni
Collection, Milan

This bracelet consists of two silver-plated stamped metal sections, joined together by a double hinge, depicting a tangle of tulip leaves and buds. The overall floral design is enclosed in a rope-patterned frame. The two bracelet sections were made from double bands: the exterior one, molded in relief, was soldered to a thick interior sheet of metal which was hand cut and smoothed. The mass-produced component, in the shape of leaves with two tulips, was soldered to the exterior relief frame. This bracelet is the product of workmanship in which mass-produced machine-molded pieces in the style of the day (the tulips and the lily are typical of Art Nouveau) are used for an object whose construction was subsequently handmade. The bending and cutting of the interior sheet, the soldering, and the hinges and clasp were all executed by hand.

BUCKLE WITH
A MEDALLION

**Place and Date
of Manufacture**
Czechoslovakia,
early 1900s

**Materials and
Techniques**
Stamped metal, part
silver and gold plate

Mark
None

Provenance
Private collection,
Vienna

Here is an example of a "transitional" jewel, that is, one bearing two styles: the neoclassical, represented by the cameo motif, and Jugendstil, seen in the naturalistic clover ornamentation. A blending of styles, sometimes successfully executed but at other times of questionable outcome, often occurs in nonprecious ornaments. In its day, the function of this type of object was to add a new touch to a dress, given that women did not change their outfits as often as they do nowadays. At the beginning of the century, an elegant woman had to have a new ornament for every hour of the day and for every occasion. Even the most traditional women, who up until a few years earlier would have refused to wear anything other than real jewelry, began to accept the idea of wearing nonprecious ornaments. Women would occassionally even wear them as substitutes for the family jewels which, if seen too often, could become boring.

This oval bracelet, in partially silver-plated and partially stamped metal, has an array of clover motifs. The imitation cameo center of the bracelet consists of a circle with a silver-colored profile of a woman against a background of gold plate.

58

BROOCH WITH BRANCHES OF MISTLETOE

Place and Date of Manufacture
Probably Germany, early 1900s

Materials and Techniques
Cast gold-plated metal, in part oxidized; glass beads

Mark
None

Provenance
Private collection, Milan

Mistletoe, as a decorative motif, occupies a privileged place in the Art Nouveau repertory of themes from nature. This motif, drawn from Victorian jewelry which had in turn taken it from the Celtic tradition (where it was considered to be a symbol of fertility), frequently recurs in French jewelry making. Interpreted in a variety of ways, mistletoe was used to embellish both gold jewelry and nonprecious ornaments. Depictions of mistletoe are also found on ornaments made in Germany. In that country, however, mistletoe has a twofold connotation. Its negative meaning derives from an ancient legend in which an arrow made from mistletoe killed the god of light. Viewed positively, it was considered a symbol of love because the tears of the slain god's wife fell on the mistletoe and changed into pearls.

This cast-metal brooch depicts two linked mistletoe branches, arranged as an irregular oval. Small glass beads nestle in the center of the partially burnished gold-plate leaves.

IRIS BROOCH

Place and Date of Manufacture
Czechoslovakia, early 1900s

Materials and Techniques
Fire-enameled stamped silver

Mark
Sterling

Provenance
Private collection, Milan

Enameling techniques date back to the ancient Egyptians, Romans, and Byzantines, who often used enamel as a substitute for precious stones. Later, the Carolingian and Romanesque workshops in the monasteries of France and Germany commonly applied enamel to their products. Enamel assumed fundamental importance in jewelry of the Victorian and Art Nouveau eras. During these periods, jewelers chose humble materials over precious stones because the former offered them greater freedom.

The two irises depicted on the brooch were enameled in shades of deep blue, ivory, yellow, and green using *basse taille*, which literally means shallow cut. This process first involves making an engraved design on a metal surface, such as silver; the surface is then covered with transparent enamel and fused by firing, resulting in rich, deep hues.

The iris, typical of Art Nouveau, expressed the eternal renewal of nature and the continuity of the life cycle through death and rebirth.

SILVER AND ENAMEL BUCKLE

When fashion calls for long, tight-waisted dresses, it follows that the waistline becomes the focal point of a woman's toilette, which was the case during the Art Nouveau years. Around 1905, belts fashioned from scarves whose ends nearly reached the ankles were in vogue. But only a year later, fashion turned back to the classic belt in its simplest form: a band fastened with a buckle. The buckle is one of the most enduring ornaments in the history of fashion. Its function as a clasp for a belt is married to the decorative style of the materials and colors used. The September 1908 issue of the magazine *Femina* proclaimed that the most beautiful buckles of the time were those in the Art Nouveau style, in silver and enamel, perfect for wearing with daytime dress or black evening wear.

Pictured above are two herons in the act of taking flight, each enclosed in an asymmetrical frame. The overall shape is that of a stylized butterfly. The two cabochon glass-paste stones simulate moonstones, evoking a star-filled sky. Traces of red and green enamel can be seen in the hollows of the birds' feathers.

Place and Date of Manufacture
Czechoslovakia, early 1900s

Materials and Techniques
Stamped, silver-plated, and partially painted metal; glass paste

Mark
None

Provenance
Private collection

LOCKET NECKLACE

Manufacturer
Fritz Rossier

**Place and Date
of Manufacture**
Cologne (Germany),
early 1900s

**Materials and
Techniques**
Embossed silver

Mark
German 800 silver
mark, F. R.

Provenance
Private collection

The locket has always been a very popular item of jewelry and especially so during Victorian times, when sentimental display was one of the prime functions of jewelry and *ex votos*, even those made in metal.

The poppy is another example of Art Nouveau's borrowing from nature. The locket shown here was made by embossing, which involves making a relief decoration by working on the reverse side of a sheet of metal with a chisel or a hammer. The locket hangs from a snake chain.

POLYCHROME ENAMELED BROOCH

The Kunstgewerbeschule of the Österreichisches Museum für Kunst und Industrie in Vienna, now the Museum für angewandte Kunst (the Museum of Fine Arts), was founded in 1867 with the goal of curbing the devastating effects of the Industrial Revolution. The founders hoped to create institutional support for individual industries and artisans' workshops by giving professional courses in various applied fields, among them jewelry and fabric design, and precious and nonprecious metalworking. Their goals were fully realized, for in addition to professional training, the school simultaneously provided an efficient distribution and support system geared to opening new markets. It was the teachers from the Kunstgewerbeschule, together with a few artists (Dagoberte Peche, Otto Lendecke, and others), who gave birth to the Wiener Werkstätte in 1903.

Manufacturer
Kunstgewerbeschule
(School of Applied Arts)
of Vienna

Place and Date of Manufacture
Austria, c. 1905

Materials and Techniques
Stamped and enameled silver

Mark
None

Provenance
Private collection, Vienna

The octagonal silver brooch pictured here is polychrome enamel. The servant figure wears a headdress and costume in white, black, and orange. In his outspread arms he holds two bunches of multicolored flowers. On either side of the figure is a pot of flowers. A dense floral mosaic in azure, orange, green, yellow, and violet serves as the background.

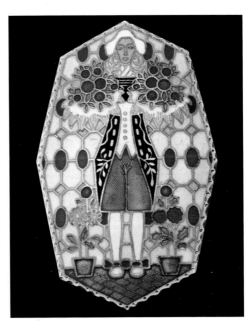

SCANDINAVIAN
TREFOIL BROOCH

This brooch is typical of Scandinavian design with its emphasis on abstracted floral patterns. The overall trefoil pattern of this gold-plated silver brooch is made of twisted and soldered metal wire. In the center of each is a pearl-like bead, also employed throughout the brooch. Small chains link each of the shields. The medium-sized shield (seen below) opens at the back and can be detached from the rest of the brooch. A round woman's watch can then be inserted inside the detachable section.

Manufacturer
Unidentified

**Place and Date
of Manufacture**
Ystas (Sweden),
early 1900s

**Materials and
Techniques**
Stamped, gold-plated
silver, twisted metal
wire, small beads

Mark
Silver mark for Ystas,
Sweden, and C.L.M.
(goldsmith)

Provenance
Veronica Guiduzzi
Collection, Bologna

VENETIAN
BEADED SAUTOIR

This sautoir is still preserved in its original case.
Although made in Italy, the box has an inscription in French, the language which traditionally evokes the world of fashion: *Verres, Perles et Mosaïques de Murano, Griffon Frères, Venice.* (The name Griffon Frères may refer to the manufacturer-distributor or only to the distributor.)

This extremely refined object is an example of the highest quality of "souvenir" jewelry. The long sautoir consists of three strands of transparent *conterie* beads alternating with yellow, pink, and green *conterie* beads. Oval lamp beads, with a light background and floral ornamentation in pink, blue, green, and yellow, are either clustered in groups of two or three different sizes or set off individually. The floral beads add overall symmetry and also serve to enliven the pallor of the *conterie* beads. A central cluster of three lamp-worked beads supports a cascade of small beads in the same shades.

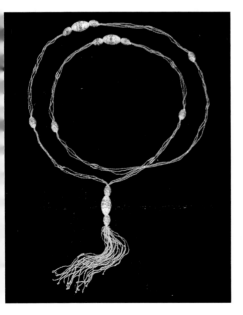

Manufacturer
Fratelli Griffon, Venice

Place and Date of Manufacture
Venice, early 1900s

Materials and Techniques
Conterie and Venetian lamp beads

Mark
None

Provenance
Costanza Fiani Collection, Milan

BROOCH WITH PENDANTS

Designer
Unidentified

Manufacturer
Theodor Fahrner

**Place and Date
of Manufacture**
Pforzheim (Germany),
1912–18

**Materials and
Techniques**
Cast black-enameled
silver, marcasite
and agate

Mark
T. F.

Provenance
Private collection

With its blend of black enamel and green agate this ogival-shaped pin seems to anticipate one of the most innovative, avant-garde color combinations of Art Deco. Along with coral and onyx this combination became popular after 1920.

The black enamel brooch with its lanceolate ornamental designs in marcasite, supports two long black enamel-and-marcasite drops and green cabochon-cut agate ovals, one at each end and a larger one in the center. This pin is now considered to be a rarity due to the recent popularity of jewelry created by Theodor Fahrner among collectors, especially those in Germany and America. The value of Fahrner's jewelry was also enhanced by the enthusiasm generated by a traveling exhibit that brought about a greater awareness of his work. The objects displayed were differentiated on the basis of materials, styles, and themes.

HAT PINS

Charles Horner, headquartered in Halifax, is the name of the English firm that first mass-produced simplified versions of Liberty jewelry, especially hat pins. At the beginning of the twentieth century, the style of tight-waisted bodices with an open or flared neck, drama-ized by wide hats on elaborate hairdos pulled back into soft chignons, was widespread. These broad-brimmed hats were attached to the hair with long hat pins. The fashion for hat pins simultaneously took hold in Berlin, Paris, London, and New York. Some pins were so long that they actu-ally presented a hazard to innocent passersby. Eventually, some coun-ries intervened and restricted the use of hat pins; an event that provoked reactions of disappointment and revolt in the world of fashion and launched the so-called "hat pin war," chronicled in the magazines at the time.

Both hat pins pictured here are silver and decorated at one end with a stylized thistle blossom made of faceted, violet-col-ored glass paste imitating amethyst. A leaflike shape finished off with a small ball supports the blossoms.

Manufacturer
Charles Horner

Place and Date of Manufacture
Chester (England), 1912

Materials and Techniques
Silver, glass paste

Mark
Mark for Chester valid for the years 1912–13, C. H.

Provenance
Virginia Fuentes Collection, New York

Art Deco:
1919–1929

GLASS-PASTE HAT PINS

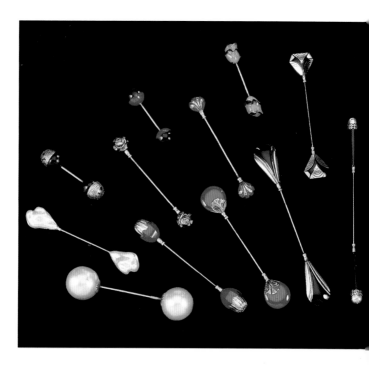

Place and Date of Manufacture
France, 1910–1930

Materials and Techniques
Glass paste, metal needles

Mark
None

Provenance
Terzo Millennio Collection, Milan

Hat pins were popular accessories in the early decades of this century. Those illustrated here are triple fired gold-plated and silver-plated glass paste, with a decoration at either end, one of which is fitted with a movable screw. Viewed as an ensemble, they give a good idea of the range of decorations in vogue—large blown-glass or faceted glass-paste stones, or fittings, also in glass paste, with undulating or floral motifs, or shaped like rounded shields or tulips shot through with sinuous glass-paste bands.

RHOMBOID PENDANT

This pendant, intended for a necklace, was cast in silver in the shape of a lozenge, embellished with an upside-down bouquet of chiseled flower petals, and partially fire enameled. The horizontal green and black enamel bands are the only strong color in the piece. This type of object is emblematic of the difficulty involved in drawing the line between nonprecious ornaments and fine jewels.

Etienne David was a jeweler who, beginning in the early years of this century, worked in Paris on the rue de la Paix, the famous avenue that drew to the area the most important jewelers, among them Cartier, Lacloche, Tiffany, and Maubassin. In addition to gold jewelry, David also produced silver ornaments which constituted his less expensive line at the time and were listed as costume jewelry. Today, however, these silver ornaments continue to fetch high prices at auctions of important jewels because of their beauty, their impeccable craftsmanship, and, above all, their evocative period style.

Therefore the question remains: Are they jewels or *bijoux*?

Designer
Etienne David

Place and Date of Manufacture
France, c. 1925

Materials and Techniques
Cast silver

Mark
E. D.

Provenance
Antichità Bersia Collection, Milan

PENDANT BROOCH IN THE SHAPE OF A VASE OF FLOWERS

Manufacturer
Unidentified

Place and Date of Manufacture
Paris, c. 1925

Materials and Techniques
Cast silver, marcasite, stamped glass paste

Mark
Paris silver mark; illegible initials of the manufacturer

Provenance
Private collection, Milan

The shape and decoration of the vase of flowers suggest that this piece may have had two sources of artistic inspiration: the severely geometrical pattern of the vase recalls the ancient Greek amphora, and the ribbonlike handles evoke decorative features typical of Chinese furniture and carpets, which often pair squared fretwork with naturalistic images. The keen interest in Chinese culture in the 1920s was largely inspired by the excavations that began in 1925 around Anyang, the capital of ancient China.

This ornament, which functions as both a brooch and a pendant, is cast silver molded in the shape of a vase with a stylized setting of flowers and leaves.

The pentagonal amphora vase is a large piece of pink glass paste, stamped with naturalistic designs. The geometric handles, the molded triangular pedestal, and the straight mouth of the vase are all made from silver and marcasite. Three glass-paste damask roses in the same shade as the vase are arranged in the middle of a bouquet of leaves made of silver and marcasite.

SAUTOIR WITH A DETACHABLE PENDANT

Place and Date of Manufacture
France, c. 1925

Materials and Techniques
Glass beads, thin metal chain, rhinestone rondelles, cast silver and rhinestone pendant

Mark
"880" (unidentified numerical mark)

Provenance
Private collection, New York

A sautoir is a long necklace that usually extends down to, or below, the waist. It was especially popular in the twenties, when its elongated lines gave a touch of femininity to the straight dresses of the time.

This sautoir consists of a single strand of green glass-paste beads strung on a chain. The beads are interspersed at regular intervals by four pierced rondelles in metal and rhinestones. A ring of blue glass at the base of the necklace is decorated on the inside with a dome and a ball in two shades of green glass paste and separated by a rhinestone rondelle.

The geometric cast silver pendant, which can be detached and used as a clip, is set with rows of châton-cut and baguette rhinestones. Three strands of green glass-paste beads, like those in the necklace, hang from the pendant. The last bead in each strand is separated from the rest by a rhinestone rondelle surmounted by a dome, the same design that adorns the inside of the blue glass ring.

SAUTOIR WITH CELLULOID PENDANT

Place and Date of Manufacture
France, c. 1925

Materials and Techniques
Molded celluloid, rhinestones, silk braid, glass-paste spheres

Mark
None

Provenance
Francine Cohen Collection, New Jersey

Plastic and its derivatives adapt very well to the simple lines and linear shapes that characterize Art Deco style, a style that conveys the modern spirit of the era. Plastic can be molded, cleaned, polished, and formed into any desired shape; it is neither precious nor costly and needs no further adornments other than its own colors. For these reasons, one can safely say that plastic jewels are among the major players in the years between 1920 and 1930.

This sautoir is composed of an orange silk braid interspersed with glass-paste ovals, simulating coral. The injection-molded red celluloid pendant, in a soft drop shape, is decorated on the front with two triangular inserts of colorless rhinestones. The elongated points of the triangles just touch the edges of a six-petaled flower. This rhinestone flower has a red glass stone in its center, repeating the ones that decorate the border of the pendant.

RED, YELLOW, AND GREEN CHOKER

This necklace is a clear indication that the beauty of an object does not necessarily arise from the precious nature of the materials used to make it, but from the idea behind its conception.

Metal bezels and cabochon glass stones are among the materials most commonly used to make jewelry; cabochons in particular are available in an infinite variety of shapes, sizes, and colors. When combined, they can give rise to a very striking object like this one, whose contrasting colors enliven the pattern while the muted tone of the oxidized silver plating moderates the overall exuberance of the vivid colors. The necklace is silver-plated metal, with cabochon-cut glass-paste stones in yellow, red, green, and blue.

The glass-paste stones, mounted in round hammered bezels, are arranged in a winding procession and follow a precise chromatic order, giving the pattern a tubular, open-work line. Two cabochon settings are soldered to either side of the tongued catch.

Place and Date of Manufacture
France, c. 1925

Materials and Techniques
Bezels soldered together to form a chain, glass-paste stones

Mark
None

Provenance
Carolle Thibaut-Pomerantz Collection, Paris

BLACK-AND-WHITE GALALITH CHOKER

Designer
Auguste Bonaz

Manufacturer
Auguste Bonaz

Place and Date of Manufacture
Oyonnax (France), c. 1925

Materials and Techniques
Handworked galalith

Mark
None

Provenance
Private collection, Paris

Black and white were employed to great effect in Art Deco design. In jewelry making, the successful pairing of ivory or diamonds with onyx or jet is largely due to the women's fashions in the twenties. Fashion ranged from Sonia Delaunay's brilliant colored fabrics, with their cubistlike designs, to more sober fabrics for sporty daytime outfits, to Paul Poiret's sumptuous evening gowns with their black-and-white designs and embroidery. The necklaces on this page and on the following page are effective examples of color pairing. The one on this page is made of two semicircular sections of tubular handworked galalith, set opposite one another in contrasting black and white. On the sides and in the center, black and white rectangular pieces break up the continuity of the tubular line. The fastener is silver-plated metal.

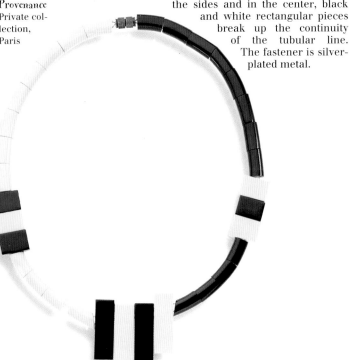

RED-AND-BLACK
GALALITH CHOKER

The chromatic exuberance of Art Deco style, in which bold polychromes are combined with contrasting pairs of primary colors and black and white, also came to dominate costume jewelry production. For example, prestigious jewelers, such as Gérard Sandoz and Boucheron, successfully paired red coral with black onyx. Also brilliant were the costumes and settings of Diaghilev's Ballets Russes, with their brilliant reds, yellows, and emerald greens and the dazzling palette of Fauvist paintings, which suggested unusual combinations of materials, often in strongly contrasting colors. This choker is composed of graduated handworked red-and-black galalith. A silver-plated fastener, consisting of a finely ribbed cylinder, finishes the piece.

Designer
Auguste Bonaz

Manufacturer
Auguste Bonaz

Place and Date of Manufacture
France, c. 1925

Materials and Techniques
Handworked bicolor galalith

Mark
None

Provenance
Private collection, Paris

SIMULATED ONYX AND CORAL SAUTOIR

Place and Date of Manufacture
France, c. 1925

Materials and Techniques
Small glass tubes, glass-paste spheres and ovals, silver-plated links

Mark
None

Provenance
Private collection, New York

The fascination with Oriental art, and with ex-oticism in general, takes on a variety of forms in the jewelry and nonprecious ornaments of the Art Deco period. Two forms predominated: the renewed use of iconography of Chinese, Persian, and Egyptian derivation; and the im-portation of colored stones already engraved with naturalistic themes and symbols. For this sautoir, lampworking produced these wound-glass imitation coral beads. The sautoir is composed of small black glass-paste cylin-ders, alternating with wound ovoid and round beads, both made from coral-colored glass paste. The ovoid beads have a ring of rhine-stones and silver-plated metal at either end. The center-piece of the sautoir consists of two more wound imita-tion coral beads, both larger than those in the body of the necklace. Small links and trim-mings on the cylin-ders, both in silver-plated metal, complete the decorative design.

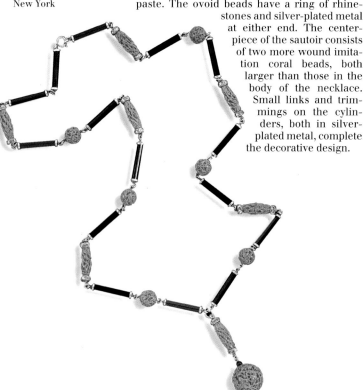

NECKLACE WITH A
RED-AND-BLACK PENDANT

This single-strand necklace is fashioned from fine silver mesh interspersed with stylized, open-work ornaments and black glass-paste cylindrical fittings. The geometric silver pendant with its sharp-edged black enamel and marcasite structure, showcases the red-enameled rectangle. Two open-work semicircles define the red rectangle. At the base of the piece, a rectangular onyx plaque with ribbonlike black enamel pieces on either side is finished with alternating bands of black enamel and marcasite. The overall form of the stacked pendant, with its clean, well-defined lines and contrasting red and black colors, suggests avant-garde art in the early years of this century.

Place and Date of Manufacture
Germany, c. 1925

Materials and Techniques
Enameled silver, marcasite, onyx

Mark
Sterling Silver Germany

Provenance
Private collection

HINGE BRACELET

Manufacturer
Kollmar & Jourdan

Place and Date of Manufacture
Pforzheim (Germany),
c. 1925

Materials and Techniques
Doublé d'or, in part
fired enamel

Mark
KJAG

Provenance
Private collection,
Milan

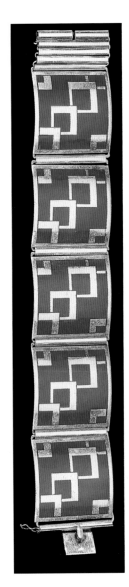

Kollmar & Jourdan was one of the largest firms in Pforzheim, Germany. Founded in 1885, it specialized in the production of gold-plated metal jewelry. In 1925, the firm employed 1,800 workers and continued to flourish until the Second World War, when their factory was destroyed in a bombardment. The factory was rebuilt and the firm continued in operation until 1977. The personal ornaments produced by Kollmar & Jourdan can be identified by their geometric lines—in which baked enamel surfaces alternate with gold-plated or silver-plated surfaces—and by their colors which are almost always drawn from Oriental culture (lacquer red, cobalt blue). This bracelet is a beautiful example of *doublé d'or*. The ornament is composed of five flexible, arched plaques, partly covered with fired blue enamel and inset with a gold plate geometric design.

PLATED RECTANGULAR BROOCH

Theodor Fahrner was one of the most important German manufacturers of costume jewelry and nonprecious ornamental objects. The firm, which was founded in 1855, participated in the Paris Exposition of 1900.

From 1900 to 1919 a number of important designers worked for this firm, among them Georg Kleeman and Joseph Maria Olbrich. Many of Fahrner's products were exported to other European countries, in particular to England, where the firm had a partnership agreement with Murrle, Benner & Co., which had offices both in Pforzheim and London.

This rectangular-shaped brooch is typical of the work produced by Fahrner. It has a carré-cut onyx mounted in the upper-left corner. Radial bands of polychrome enamel in shades of green, white, red, and violet are divided into segments. Every other segment is studded with raised, grooved wire. The bottom and one of the side edges are finished with a cordonlike molding.

Manufacturer
Theodor Fahrner

Place and Date of Manufacture
Pforzheim (Germany), c. 1928

Materials and Techniques
Enameled silver, braided wire

Mark
T. F.

Provenance
Private collection

CHROME-PLATED METAL BROOCH

Manufacturer
Jakob Bengel

Place and Date of Manufacture
Idar Oberstein (Germany), c. 1930

Materials and Techniques
Chain, chrome-plated metal, galalith

Mark
None

Provenance
Private collection

In the many books devoted to the subject of costume jewelry and objects made from plastics, the makers of charming ornaments made from chrome and galalith, objects characterized by the marked color contrast between the plastic (red, blue, green, or black) and the chrome, are often listed as "anonymous." However, we now know that the manufacturer of at least some of these objects was Jakob Bengel. This identification was made possible by the discovery in 1993 (the same year in which Bengel's firm ceased operations) of books containing the designs for the objects manufactured in their factory. The firm, established in 1871, initially produced watch chains In the period from 1930–39, the firm became a producer of fashion accessories exported to France and the United States. Their most sought-after products, examples of perfect Deco style, are necklaces made from galalith, or glass, and chrome.

The necklace shown below, in chrome-plated cast metal, comprising slender tubes alternating with small balls, is a typical example of Bengel's output. The central leaf-shaped pendant is in two shades of azure galalith. Four deep hatches, representing the veins of the leaf, end in circular studs. The two spheres adjoining the necklace and the pendant reprise the round shape of the studs.

MARCASITE BROOCH

Manufacturer
Theodor Fahrner

**Place and Date
of Manufacture**
Pforzheim (Germany),
c. 1930

**Materials and
Techniques**
Cast silver, marcasite,
amazonite

Mark
Superimposed TF; 935

Provenance
Private collection

The firm of Theodore Fahrner manufactured jewelry in an extremely rich variety of designs and styles from 1855 until 1979, when the business finally closed down. Over the course of its production, a multitude of materials (gold, silver, nickel silver, gold-plated metal, semi-precious stones), genres, subjects, and types of workmanship bear the TF mark. However, because so many designers worked for the firm, it is nearly impossible to determine the paternity of an individual pattern without consulting the technical-scientific catalogue that was published in 1990, on the occasion of the exhibit dedicated to Fahrner's production.

This brooch is cast silver and marcasite molded in the shape of a drop, adorned in the center with two vertically aligned amazonite stones, one square-shaped and the other curved. A semicircular shape, broken by four curved amazonite stones, forms the base of the brooch.

SAUTOIR WITH YELLOW-TONED BEADS

Manufacturer
Unknown, probably for
the Wiener Werkstätte

**Place and Date
of Manufacture**
Vienna, c. 1920–25

**Materials and
Techniques**
Papier-maché balls,
crocheted small glass
beads

Mark
None

Provenance
Private collection,
Milan

This type of necklace, known as "Vienna Beads" and made of small glass beads covering papier-maché balls, is very much sought after in the vintage jewelry market since most of these necklaces were produced by the Wiener Werkstätte in limited editions. We know that Felice Rix, a female designer and, therefore, a true rarity in the early years of the century designed most of these pieces. The main part of this piece is a long rope of colored beads in orange, gray, and white. The colors are blended so as to create different chromatic nuances and patterns.

One end of the necklace has five beaded balls (two orange, two orange and yellow, one ocher and yellow), while the other end has six (two orange, two orange and yellow, one ocher and yellow, and one yellow).

COLORED TUBULAR SAUTOIR

The glass beads used in this necklace were made in Gablonz (now Jablonec Nad Nisou, in the Czech Republic) where, beginning in the Renaissance, generation after generation of artisans have specialized in glass-working.

For centuries missionaries, explorers, and merchants took glass beads with them on their travels to be used as gifts or barter. Beads were often bartered in Africa—in exchange for ivory, gold, and slaves—and in North America. The Great Lakes Indians took the beads, in exchange for tobacco and silver, to decorate their clothing and ceremonial headdresses.

Necklaces of the type reproduced here generally have contrasting colors: soft shades like ivory or ocher, or bright tones like orange and cobalt blue exist side by side in a single ornament fashioned from humble but highly decorative materials. The long ropy necklace is predominantly of black glass beads, interspersed with white, gray, cobalt blue, and azure beads crocheted together, used either alone or mixed with other colors to create a variety of chromatic and visual effects. Each end of the slender bead rope is finished with a ball, one black and the other orange, with minor beading in white.

Manufacturer
Unknown, probably for the Wiener Werkstätte

Place and Date of Manufacture
Vienna, c. 1920–25

Materials and Techniques
Papier-maché balls, small glass beads

Mark
None

Provenance
Private collection, New York

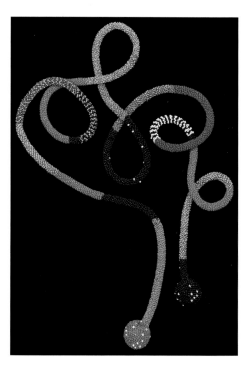

ENVELOPE BROOCH

Place and Date of Manufacture
Austria, c. 1925

Materials and Techniques
Stamped and enameled silver, marcasite

Mark
Austria

Provenance
Private collection

Austrian Art Deco production, with its austere, concise shapes, is perfectly consistent with the functionalism of the Wiener Werkstätte whose work has been said to be "of an angular, geometric, and square beauty." These products call to mind the influence of cubist, expressionist, and abstract art.

The Bauhaus also decisively influenced the style of Austrian nonprecious jewelry. With its deliberately exaggerated simplicity, the new jewelry liberated itself from the traditions of gold jewelry and declared its independence. These nonprecious jewels also took on a specific decorative function, brief and transitory though it may be, that has its origin in color rather than form.

An example is this stamped-silver rectangular brooch, divided into four triangles and enameled in black, red, yellow, and green. The center of the pin is decorated with three rows of faceted marcasite. Clear brilliant marcasite, a variety of pyrite that is subsequently polished and faceted, has a metallic gray color that is particularly suited to being paired with variously colored enameled materials.

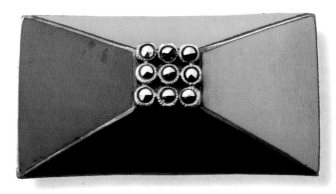

ENGRAVED WOOD BROOCH

In an article that appeared in *Schmuck, Zeichen am Korper* in 1967, Peter Weibel, an important writer on the decorative arts, stated: "classical jewelry is anonymous elegance [whereas] the terribly monotonous routine of prestige [is] a residue of sentimentality." This assertion is well suited to the evolution undertaken by Austrian jewelry makers following the lessons of the Wiener Werkstätte: a quality object need not defer to external values, rather it can stand on its own.

This rectangular wood-and-silver brooch depicts hand-engraved geometrical designs on a silver mounting. The accordionlike band is set off by two silver lateral bars, each adorned with two triangles in counterpoint.

Even though the material used for the brooch is rather ordinary, the workmanship, carried out entirely by hand, is impeccable. The two side pieces, with their pure geometric shapes, are perfect evidence of both the excellence of the craftsmanship and of the style of the era.

Designer
H. Kleiss

Manufacturer
H. Kleiss

Place and Date
of Manufacture
Austria, c. 1928

Materials and
Techniques
Silver, wood

Mark
H. Kleiss

Provenance
Private collection

BROOCHES WITH
WATCH PENDANTS

C. BUCHERER

Manufacturer
2. C. Bucherer

**Place and Date
of Manufacture**
1. & 2. Probably
Germany;
3. Probably France.
All made, c. 1930

**Materials and
Techniques**
Silver and metal,
marcasite

Mark
1. None; 2. "925,"
Swiss import stamp
for the early 1900s,
C. Bucherer; 3. Sterling

Provenance
Private collection,
Milan

Watch pendants, in a variety of designs, were common at the beginning of the century. One of the most frequently employed decorative styles was *guilloché* enameling (the use of a machine-turned lathe on metal, producing a variety of patterns) and plant motifs in diamonds (or rhinestones in imitation jewelry) on a monochrome background, a style perfectly suited to the garland style of the time.

Also dating from the same period as these brooches is the lorgnette, a single or double opera glass, whose lenses can be fit into grooves in the handle and hung on a chain like a pendant. The lorgnette clearly derives from the Victorian chatelaine, on which a woman hung implements for work or for repairing her toilette. The lorgnette reached the height of its glory in the Art Nouveau period. The sinuous lines of that era were suited to the rounded shape of this type of ornament with its wide variety of frames in bone, tortoise shell, and horn, in addition to the ones made from metal inlaid with mother-of-pearl and real or imitation stones.

PENDANT WITH A LARGE YELLOW STONE

This is an extremely beautiful example of perfect Art Deco style in which the geometric lines of the frame set off the huge stone to just the right degree. A stone of this extraordinary size is easily made from glass for a piece of costume jewelry, but is rarely found in nature. A real stone like this one would only be used in jewels of enormous value destined for an elite class of buyers.

The pendant is silver, in a molded rectangular shape, with a large, octagonal-cut, faceted stone of orange-yellow glass, simulating topaz. The silver frame is worked with a decorative design in relief, studded with marcasite. Set into the frame are green glass-paste baguettes, simulating amazonite, and faceted amethyst-colored stones. The bail of the pendant has smooth corners and a violet-colored stone in the center. Three rectangular sections, arranged stepwise and set with alternating violet and green glass-paste baguettes, join the pendant to the bail.

Place and Date of Manufacture
Czechoslovakia, c. 1925

Materials and Techniques
Cast silver, faceted stones, glass-paste stones, marcasite

Mark
Mark for silver objects imported from Czechoslovakia, Sterling 935

Provenance
Private collection, Milan

DRESS CLIPS

Place and Date of Manufacture
Czechoslovakia,
c. 1920–1930

Materials and Techniques
Glass paste, stamped
and galvanized with a
triple-fired silver color

Mark
None

Provenance
Private collection,
Milan

In their totality, these clips exemplify typical
Art Deco shapes—geometric and stylized, with
strong, harmonious colors. Clips were the perfect adornment for the dresses of the day. The
prevailing fashion was straight and followed
the shape of the body; a shape that was only
occasionally broken by the odd fold or a cluster
of darts at the hips or in the center of the skirt.
A clip was placed at strategic points, such as
where draping was formed by the folds or
darts or at the bottom of the neckline. Clips
could be as shiny as diamonds, or colored like
the ones seen here, in geometrical shapes
made from glass paste in a variety of colors,
including blue, green, white, red, yellow, or
gray, and decorated with veining or inserts. In
the forties, clips experienced another upsurge
in popularity as a decoration for the square
neckline which had come back into fashion.

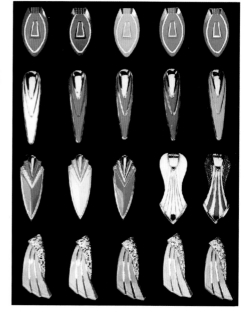

CHATELAINE-STYLE DOUBLE CLIPS

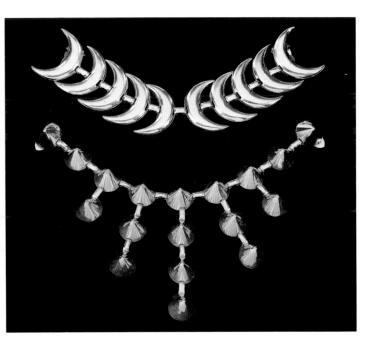

Finding an example of a nonprecious ornament made in Italy before the end of the Second World War is very difficult, if not virtually impossible. The only thing we can say with certainty is that costume jewelry did exist at the time in Italy because manufacturers were regularly represented at the triennials and decorative arts expositions. Both of the models above are chatelaine-style, the one on top formed by ten rounded, smooth crescent moons, five on each side, turned away from each other. The crescents are connected by flexible links. The clip consists of cone-shaped metal arranged like a fringe. Small flexible links connect the cones; the fasteners are composed of two clips. The overall rational, though modest design, and at least for Italy, innovative materials, reflect the influence of the Bauhaus.

Place and Date of Manufacture
Italy, c. 1930

Materials and Techniques
Stamped, chrome-plated metal

Mark
None

Provenance
Private collection, Milan

GALALITH SAUTOIR
WITH PENDANT

Manufacturer
E. A. Bliss Co.

**Place and Date
of Manufacture**
United States, c. 1920

**Materials and
Techniques**
Galalith, gold-plated
metallic findings

Mark
Bliss (on one of the
metallic components)

Provenance
Lo Scrigno del
Tempo Collection,
Avellino, Italy

The mark stamped "Bliss" on one of the three metallic components of the necklace leads one to believe that this sautoir is the work of the E. A. Bliss Co., headquartered in Connecticut. The company was founded by E. A. Bliss and J. E. Carpenter in 1875 when the Whitney & Rice Co., the firm that Bliss worked for at the time, was taken over. E. A. Bliss moved to Connecticut in 1891 and in 1893 began to manufacture gift articles and personal ornaments in silver. In 1922 the firm's trade name was changed to the Napier Co., after the company's president H. Napier, who held this post until 1960.

The sautoir is formed of four elongated triangular units, alternating with two stylized bows, fastened to black galalith rods interspersed with cream-colored ovals. The center of the bows are cream colored, intended to simulate ivory. Galalith balls highlight the components that make up the front of the necklace. The galalith pendant has an open-work center.

LARGE OWL BROOCH

Manufacturer
Staret

**Place and Date
of Manufacture**
Chicago, c. 1941

**Materials and
Techniques**
Cast rhodium-plated
metal, partially
enameled in black;
rhinestones

Mark
Staret

Provenance
Robin Feldman
Collection, New York

STARET Since time immemorial, the owl has been associated with the mystery and hidden powers of nature and with death. Its presence is thought to be a harbinger of the spiritual world. It is also one of the most common subjects for jewelry.

The brooch pictured on this page depicts an owl's head in châton-cut rhinestones separated by linear bands of black enamel, arranged so as to outline the bird's features. The eyes are made from two faceted carré-cut red-glass stones.

The design of this brooch, with its severely geometric stylized lines, emphasizes the lasting influence of Art Deco style in the United States. As late as the forties, jewelry and ornaments revealed their formal Art Deco heritage, even as they began to exhibit the naturalistic themes of the years to come. In fact, these two sources of inspiration could be combined to create a well-balanced whole.

NECKLACE WITH LAPIS LAZULI

Manufacturer
Napier

Place and Date of Manufacture
United States, 1925–30

Materials and Techniques
Stamped silver-plated metal, lapis lazuli

Mark
Napier

Provenance
Antichità De Giovanni Collection, Milan

The Napier Co., headquartered in Meriden, Connecticut, is one of the few illustrious businesses of the twenties, thirties, and forties that still exists today. The success of this company is due to its tailored jewelry, made of gold- or silver-plated metal without any stones. It is sober in style and is primarily suited for wearing in the daytime by the kind of woman who likes something special but doesn't want to call attention to herself.

The lapis lazuli necklace shown here is just such an example. It is made of small hexagonal plates in silver-plated stamped metal, separated by oval links. The plates are decorated with stylized embossed flowers. The trilobed pendant is of silver-plated stamped metal with embossed stylized and ribbed decorations. Faceted lapis lazuli, mounted in a hammered setting, makes up the center of the pendant.

This necklace was shown at the exhibit "All That Glitters," held at the Bass Museum of Art in Miami Beach from December 18, 1994 to February 2, 1995.

NECKLACE WITH AN OPEN-WORK PENDANT

Fishel, Nessler & Co., in operation from 1893 to 1937, had its headquarters in New York. The firm specialized in the manufacture of rhinestone and silver ornaments. This necklace is a single strand of glass simulated pearls, alternating with vivid red fluted balls. The pattern of alternating balls and pearls is varied by four jeweled cylinders, made from metal covered with baguette-cut rhinestones and finished with two rounded metal and rhinestone units.

The geometric pendant, of cast open-work silver, has a floral theme made up of châton-cut rhinestones. The uppermost section of the pendant is Oriental in style, with carré-cut and rhinestone baguettes.

Manufacturer
Fishel, Nessler & Co.

Place and Date of Manufacture
United States, c. 1930

Materials and Techniques
Simulated pearls, glass balls, cast metal covered with rhinestones

Mark
Fishel Sterling

Provenance
Private collection, Milan

The White Period—
The First Costume Jewelry: 1930–1939

SAUTOIR
WITH PENDANT

Manufacturer
Unidentified

**Place and Date
of Manufacture**
Austria, c. 1930

**Materials and
Techniques**
Crystal stones, silver

Mark
935 (fineness), import
stamp for France,
J. K. in an oval field
(goldsmith)

Provenance
Private collection,
Milan

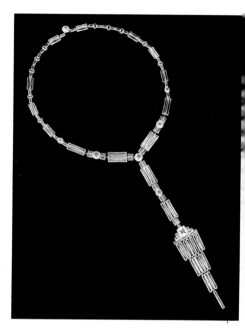

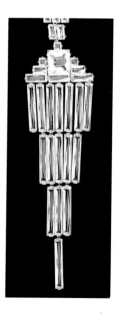

In the film *Weekend in Havana*, Joan Crawford
wore a sautoir in the same shape as the one
pictured here. Hers, however, was more than
likely made from precious stones, since in the
thirties the most important French and American jewelers competed with one another to
lend their jewelry to the stars of Hollywood.
The jewelers believed that the loan would be
more than compensated for by increased sales
of their jewels.

This necklace is a sautoir composed of
geometric units of clear crystal in silver prong
settings with an open back. The extraordinary
pendant is enhanced by a large brilliant-cut
crystal in the center.

CUPOLA-SHAPED HANGING EARRINGS

Few objects combine the geometric shapes of Art Deco style with the fashion for white in the thirties to greater effect than this pair of earrings. After the contrasting color palette of preceding years, fashion in the thirties called for dresses and jewelry in clear and brilliant white.

The upper part of these open-work silver earrings is a double rose fashioned from eight spirals of châton stones set with a larger rhinestone in the center. A trefoil of châtons supports a cupola outlined by arched bands of pavé-set rhinestones interspersed with three rows of rhinestone solitaires and a pair of rhinestone leaves. A loose fringe continues the decorative patterns of the cupola.

Manufacturer
Unidentified

Place and Date of Manufacture
Paris, c. 1930

Materials and Techniques
Worked silver, rhinestones

Mark
Paris silver mark and illegible initials of the manufacturer in a lozenge-shaped field

Provenance
Carolle Thibaut-Pomerantz Collection, Paris

CONVERTIBLE BROOCH

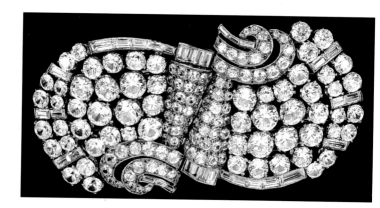

Manufacturer
Unidentified

Place and Date of Manufacture
Paris, c. 1930

Materials and Techniques
Silver, rhinestones

Mark
Paris silver mark; "Ste ZS" in a lozenge-shaped field (unidentified initials of the manufacturer)

Provenance
Private collection, Paris

This brooch, which can be converted into two clips, is in perfect accord with the trend in thirties jewelry in which the brilliance of diamonds substitutes for color. A combination of brilliant-cut and châton-cut stones creates a varied play of white light. The brooch's fluid line lightens the geometric severity of Art Deco and anticipates the abstract and naturalistic shapes of the forties—spirals, curls, feathers, and wreaths—which were interpreted with moderation in France, and more strikingly in the United States. Each of the brooch clips has a rounded line with a conical pattern of pavé-set châtons and baguettes. When joined together to form a brooch, the clips produce an imposing, sumptuous object. However, individually, the clips have an effect and are of a size that falls within the norms for jewelry in those days.

RHINESTONE AND GLASS-STONE BRACELET

Manufacturer
Unidentified

**Place and Date
of Manufacture**
Germany, c. 1930

**Materials and
Techniques**
Silver, rhinestones,
glass stones

Mark
0925 54, K.P.
(goldsmith)

Provenance
Private collection,
New York

This is an extremely beautiful example of a *bijou d'imitation*. Each detail is carefully studied in order to recapture the preciousness of the material used in the original jewel (platinum, diamonds, and sapphires) and is carried out with the same degree of care and precision.

This silver bracelet is banded and somewhat flexible. It is composed of six different segments, three on each side, that complement the central band which is formed of seven rows of imitation faceted stones simulating sapphires, three rows of clear baguettes, and a rectangular area of pavé-set rhinestones.

LINK BRACELET

Manufacturer
Unidentified

**Place and Date
of Manufacture**
Austria, c. 1930

**Materials and
Techniques**
Open-work cast
silver, glass paste

Mark
"935," "WB" in a
hexagonal field
(goldsmith)

Provenance
Private collection,
Venice

Black onyx and red coral are a common Art Deco combination. The tendency to use a wider variety of colors than in the past can also be found in nonprecious ornaments that opened up the field to include imitations of such semiprecious stones as coral, onyx, agate, carnelian, lapis lazuli, and so forth.

This bracelet is cast openwork silver, with rhinestones forming six rectangular garlanded units ending in florid rosettes. Three glass-paste cabochons in the middle of each unit are appliquéd in a diagonal line, with a black stone, imitating onyx, in the center and a red stone, imitating coral, to either side. The surrounding pavé-set rhinestones create a white background which offsets the deep black onyx and blazing red coral.

BAR BROOCH WITH PENDANT

The bar brooch, consisting of an oblong clip and a pendant, enjoyed particular success in the twenties and thirties. All of the great jewelers, from Mouboussin to Cartier, Fouquet, and Van Cleef & Arpels, created beautiful examples of this kind of brooch. The design in the center of the pendant was frequently a plant or a gushing fountain. Bar and pendant decorations on *minaudières* also appeared on evening bags made from enameled metal, most often in black. This bar brooch, in open-work silver, is fashioned from two parallel rows of châton-cut rhinestones, joined together at either end by a rhinestone mounted in a lozenge-shaped setting and bordered by two faceted carré stones whose green color simulates emeralds. The barrette supports a delicately open-worked pendant depicting a floral design, including a vase of flowers in the center. The flowers are made from small round green stones. A rectangular frame of larger rhinestones surrounds the open-work design.

Place and Date of Manufacture
Probably Germany, c. 1930

Materials and Techniques
Open-work silver, rhinestones, faceted stones

Mark
Sterling; "ster" in a serrated field

Provenance
Private collection, New York

RHINESTONE SAUTOIR
WITH DROP PENDANT

**Place and Date
of Manufacture**
Italy, c. 1930

**Materials and
Techniques**
Crystal stones, à jour
settings, silver-plated
metal

Mark
None

Provenance
Anna Valfré di Bonzo
Collection, Turin

This necklace suggests the connection between jewelry making in the early decades of
the twentieth century and the avant-garde art
movements of the late nineteenth and early
twentieth centuries. In particular, its light style
and linear, stylized shape suggest the design
principles of the Viennese Secession.

This rivière, made from seventy-eight
châton-cut crystals, has stamped silver-plated
metal links and à jour settings, which allow
light to pass through the stones, giving it great
brilliance and delicacy. A faceted crystal oval
makes up the pendant.

RHODIUM-PLATED METAL PARURE

Designer
Alfred Philippe

Manufacturer
Trifari, Krussman & Fishel, Inc.

Place and Date of Manufacture
United States, c. 1935

Materials and Techniques
Cast rhodium-plated metal, rhinestones, glass paste

Mark
Trifari

Provenance
Private collection, New York

Alfred Philippe was a designer of French descent who had previously worked for Scheer Inc., a firm that produced jewelry for both Cartier and Van Cleef & Arpels, before moving to Trifari, Krussman & Fishel. Philippe's designs were largely responsible for the enormous success of the latter. From 1930 to 1970, the firm created a huge array of costume jewelry at a level that has yet to be surpassed.

Philippe's designs for Cartier are obvious in this parure, made from cast rhodium-plated metal and gems cut in the shape of flowers. Graceful, stylized rhinestone pairings make up the necklace, with the center enhanced by stamped glass-paste flowers and fruits. The same design is also in the brooch, which can be separated into two clips. The overall shape of the brooch is rhodium-plated metal and bâton- and baguette-cut rhinestones. The matching earrings each have three stamped glass-paste stones (red, green, and blue), interspersed with individually mounted rhinestones.

BROOCH IN THE SHAPE OF A BULLDOG'S HEAD

Place and Date of Manufacture
United States, c. 1930

Materials and Techniques
Cast rhodium-plated metal, rhinestones, glass-paste stones

Mark
None

Provenance
Antichità De Giovanni Collection, Milan

As portraiture continues to exist in the realm of painting, so the tradition of reproducing subjects that are gratifying to look at or that evoke our feelings remains alive in jewelry making. Of course, one of these subjects is man's perennial best friend, the dog.

This brooch originated from metal cast in the shape of a bulldog's head. The shape and markings in the face are defined by a series of clearly delineated bands sprinkled with châton-cut rhinestones, giving the brooch a stylized open-work look, illuminated by the two glass-paste red cabochons for the eyes.

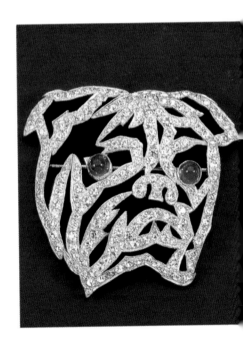

SAUTOIR WITH OPALESCENT GLASS BEADS

The main feature of this sautoir is made up of three graduated strands of opalescent glass beads in two shades of pink, interspersed with rhinestones and clear crystals. Joining the strands are two rows of opaque white crystal and small Venetian glass beads. The back part of the necklace consists of a single strand of nine rose-colored opalescent glass beads. Hanging from the sautoir is a partial strand of pink and transparent crystal beads.

This type of thin metal chain is called "Parisian." Since it was so much stronger than waxed cotton thread, which was generally used around this time, it was considered preferable for the heavy glass beads.

Place and Date of Manufacture
France, c. 1925

Materials and Techniques
Glass beads, metallic chain, small Venetian glass beads, rhinestone rondelles, crystals

Mark
None

Provenance
Private collection, New York

TWELVE-STRAND SAUTOIR

Place and Date of Manufacture
France, c. 1925

Materials and Techniques
Small glass beads, glass paste, metal and rhinestone rondelles

Mark
None

Provenance
Lo Scrigno del Tempo Collection, Avellino, Italy

Beads with this small a diameter are no longe available. Moreover, one can only rarely find sautoir like this one so perfectly preservec with the string in good condition and withou the gaps that often result from the weigh and friction of the stones. Imitation beads fre quently peel or turn dark from contact with th skin.

The centerpiece of the necklace is fou green glass-paste beads stamped with obliqu grooves, separated by three metal-and-rhine stone rondelles.

BANGLE WITH COMPACT

This bracelet was found in its original box with a picture of Josephine Baker's face, her signature, and the name of one of her films, *Zouzou* from 1934, on the inside. The bracelet appears to be a piece of costume jewelry created as a promotional device for the film, given the fact that another bracelet, also from Flamand and with the same picture, signature, and film title, was described in 1988 by C. Davidor and R. G. Dawes in *The Bakelite Book*. This double-purpose bracelet is made up of a large band surmounted by black Bakelite, with a brass insert that hides a compartment for a compact.

Manufacturer
Flamand

Place and Date of Manufacture
Paris, 1934

Materials and Techniques
Handworked black Bakelite and brass

Mark
Deposé Flamand Paris

Provenance
Private collection, New York

COLLAR
WITH BIRDS

Manufacturer
Degorge for Chanel

**Place and Date
of Manufacture**
Paris, 1936

**Materials and
Techniques**
Cast gold-plated metal

Mark
None

Provenance
Private collection

This necklace depicts two birds with outspread wings, placed on either side of a border of roses. A pendant of three lanceolate leaves with relief veining hangs from a ring. The necklace itself is composed of roses, pomegranates, and stylized leaves in gold-plated metal. The metal has been gilded, giving it the patina of "age."

This necklace can be found on page 116 of *Jewelry by Chanel* by Patrick Mauriès, published in London by Thames and Hudson in 1993. An identical necklace appeared in *La Donna* for January/February 1946 under the name Giuliano Fratti, demonstrating how much Italian fashion in those years depended on French creators.

NECKLACE OF
THREE CIRCLETS OF LEAVES

Manufacturer
Unknown, for Elsa
Schiaparelli

**Place and Date
of Manufacture**
Paris, 1936

**Materials and
Techniques**
Anitqued gold-plated
metal mesh and
components

Mark
None

Provenance
Private collection

Three circlets of metallic mesh support shoots
of lanceolate, gold-plated, pinkish-brown-
colored leaves. The necklace fastens with a
hinged clasp. *Harper's Bazaar* published this
necklace in their December 1937 issue. At a
time when jewelry tended to be more massive,
Schiaparelli preferred playful themes, such as
her famous circus collection of 1937, or naturalistic subjects that were representational,
but which had her special finishing touches. In
this case, it is the antiqued gilding that makes
this necklace worthy of note. This touch calls
to mind Schiaparelli's constant search for
something different from the usual trends of
the moment.

PINK-AND-GREEN
CHATELAINE BROOCH

Manufacturer
Unknown, perhaps
for Elsa Schiaparelli

**Place and Date
of Manufacture**
Probably France,
c. 1938

**Materials and
Techniques**
Cast metal, imitation
stones, brass spheres

Mark
None

Provenance
Private collection

This brooch has been attributed to Elsa Schiaparelli because of its humorous style and vivid
colors: shocking pink combined with green
was the hallmark of this great artist of fashion
who knew how to draw out the best from
her collaborators including Jean Clement,
Jean Schlumberger, Roger Jean-Pierre (who
became the honorary president of the Chambre Syndicale des
Paruriers de la
Haute Couture in
the eighties), and
Lyda Coppola.

This fountain
shaped brooch
painted in shock-
ing pink and aqua-
marine tones, is
composed, at the
top, of a circle
adorned with five
red glass cabo-
chon stones and
a faceted yellow
oval in the center.
Hanging from the
brooch are three
ducklings encir-
cling an aquama-
rine-colored ball.
Each duckling has
a small gold-plated
ball hanging from
its neck. Directly
below is a two-
piece mushroom,
again with small
hanging gold-plat-
ed balls, with a cap
embellished by two
faceted glass stones,
one yellow and one
red.

PARURE WITH IVY DECORATION

A French peasant legend holds that a love-stricken young girl must always have one or more ivy leaves near her heart so that her boyfriend will choose to marry her. Whether or not this legend gave rise to this suite, it is a fact that ivy often occurs as a charming source of inspiration for a decorative theme, especially in Victorian jewelry. It is considered to be the preeminent symbol of fidelity and matrimony.

What stands out in this parure is precisely the ivy-shaped ornamentation. The bracelet is a slightly convex, rigid band, in gold-plated metal and black enamel strewn with appliquéd gold-plated ivy leaves. Each leaf is embellished with three colorless châton-cut rhinestones with a glass-paste cabochon in the center, in silvery shades imitating a moonstone. The matching round pin, also slightly convex, in gold-plated metal and black enamel, reprises the same decorative motif as the bracelet.

Manufacturer
Unknown, for Elsa Schiaparelli

Place and Date of Manufacture
Probably France, c. 1937–40

Materials and Techniques
Cast in gold-plated metal and cold-enameled, glass and glass-paste stones, gold-plated metallic components

Mark
Schiaparelli

Provenance
Private collection, Vienna

SCHIAPARELLI

SAUTOIR OF
RHINESTONE COROLLAS

Designer
Unknown

**Place and Date
of Manufacture**
France, 1930–40

**Materials and
Techniques**
Rhinestones, glass
spheres, silk thread

Mark
None

Provenance
Private collection, Paris

Settings for mounting stones come in a variety of models, each of which is designed to create a certain effect when the stone is mounted. In the case of this necklace, each rhinestone is inserted into a setting with a ring-shaped stem so that the stone can then be strung on a thin cord. The resulting visual impression is one of "corollas" of radially placed rhinestones strung to form a tube. Stones set in this fashion, unlike those set in soldered mountings, are not fixed in place, rather they are movable and thus have greater dynamism.

The châton-cut rhinestones are highlighted at regular intervals by compressed balls of red glass and matte-glass stones imitating pink quartz. The sautoir, designed to be knotted in the middle, has two strands ending in small rhinestone clusters. The clusters hang from small red glass beads, connected to green silk thread. The clasp is adorned with three compressed glass beads, two red and one green, separated by small rhinestone rings.

SAUTOIR WITH GREEN GLASS STONES

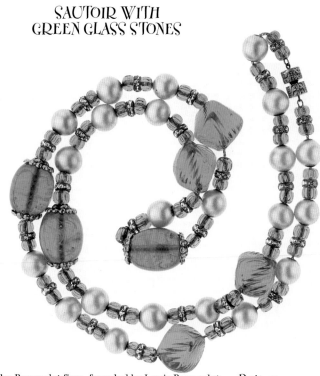

The Rousselet firm, founded by Louis Rousselet in 1919, specialized in the manufacture of glass pearls. The firm's activity broadened in the years between 1920 and 1925, when Mistinguett, the queen of the Paris Casino, became one of its most loyal customers. In those years, Rousselet provided jobs for eight hundred workers dedicated to the manufacture of simulated pearls and costume jewelry for performances at the Folies-Bergère and the Moulin Rouge. Many of Rousselet's most elaborate patterns were exclusive orders for Patou, Chanel, Heim, Fath, Paquin, Schiaparelli, and Balmain.

This sautoir is composed of simulated pearls in glass, alternating with pairs of small flattened, grooved, green glass beads separated by rhinestones. Seven larger green glass stones, either smooth with burnished metal caps or grooved and shaped like a die, are set at regular intervals. The screw clasp is engraved metal.

Designer
Louis Rousselet

Manufacturer
Louis Rousselet

Place and Date of Manufacture
Paris, 1930–40

Materials and Techniques
Simulated pearls, glass beads, metal and rhinestone rondelles, thin metal chain, metal caps and clasp

Mark
None

Provenance
Private collection

PAIR OF GALALITH
COSTUME-JEWELRY BROOCHES

**Place and Date
of Manufacture**
France, c. 1930–40

**Materials and
Techniques**
Handworked galalith,
stamped sheet of metal

Mark
None

Provenance
Costanza Fiani
Collection, Milan

Inventions and technological advances often
have their origins in external factors. In the
United States, the Great Depression created a
need for inexpensive materials that could be
easily worked by unskilled workers at little
cost, and that were also pleasing to the eye.
And so the invention of plastic, which dated
back to the nineteenth century, was now ex-
ploited to its maximum potential.

This pair of brooches, with their curved
contours, were molded in an open-work, lacy
design from carved salmon-pink galalith. The
base was made from a sheet of gold-plated
metal stamped in relief. A highly stylized
smooth bow in black galalith acts as the fastener for the brooch.

MULTICOLORED CELLULOID BROOCHES

Beginning in the early part of the twentieth century, plastic materials were no longer restricted to imitating natural substances; instead, they acquired a new potential derived from the material's inherent properties: color and brilliance. These brooches are a good example of how, in those years, plastic objects were no longer destined to imitate materials existing in nature. Rather, they were designed to represent artificiality at its best.

Eight small hollow celluloid cylinders, in red, azure, brown, yellow, and green tones, were appliquéd to the black and azure circular celluloid brooches. The other smaller two brooches are fashioned from three cup-shaped bowls arranged in a cloverleaf pattern. The cups contain small four-petaled celluloid flowers in shades of pink, yellow, green, red, white, and orange. The pistils are made from rhinestones.

Place and Date of Manufacture
France, c. 1930–40

Materials and Techniques
Multicolored molded plastic

Mark
None

Provenance
Antichità De Giovanni Collection, Milan

CIRCULAR BROOCHES

Place and Date of Manufacture
France, late 1930s

Materials and Techniques
Molded plastics, stamped metal

Mark
None

Provenance
Private collection, Paris

This group of brooches is another example of how plastics were used in a creative and diverse fashion in the United States, where they were particularly well liked during the twenties and thirties, as well as in France, the center of fashion.

The brooch above depicts an Egyptian head in profile, with a headdress and ornaments in shades of orange, dark green, and blue. The palmettes framing the profile are in the same colors and are bordered by a bicolor hatched band.

Of the three brooches at left, the top one is characterized by a cruciform motif, with ribbing and open-work ovals nearer the center. The triangular partitions are smooth, with three-petaled flowers in a lighter shade of red. The middle pin is an amberlike acetate with a smooth outer band, depicting three scarabs with outspread wings and stylized lilies. Below, the stamped-metal circular brooch has an abstract decoration of two semicircles.

WILD WEST
BROOCH AND NECKLACE

The inspiration for this necklace and brooch goes back to the legends of the Wild West that have played such a significant role in American culture. Manufacturers of both precious and nonprecious ornaments were greatly fascinated by the iconographic symbols of that conquered soil—cowboys, Indians, cactus, and exotic animals.

The brooch depicts the profile of an Indian, in light chestnut-brown Bakelite, wearing a feather headdress painted in shades of green, azure, white, pink, red, and yellow. The headdress is held in place by a string of small glass beads. A yellow-painted cloth with azure, ivory, and black decorations rests on the Indian's breast. The necklace, a wine-red celluloid chain, has partially painted charms in a variety of materials (wood, metal, celluloid, ribbon, and leather). The charms reflect the Wild West: wagon wheels, trunks, canteens, cowboy hat, a boot, and the inevitable pistol.

Place and Date of Manufacture
United States, c. 1930

Materials and Techniques
Celluloid chain, Bakelite, wood, metal, cotton ribbon, leather

Mark
None

Provenance
Private collection, New York

COLLAR, BRACELET, AND BROOCH PARURE

Place and Date of Manufacture
United States, c. 1930

Materials and Techniques
Carved and painted wood and bone

Mark
AJH Rolled gold (on the bar of the brooch)

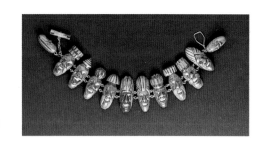

AJH ROLLEDGOLD

Provenance
Private collection

The beneficial effects of making crafts has been known for many years; invalids have often been encouraged to make ceramic objects or decorative jewelry to help with their convalescence. Such is the case with this parure, which was made either by invalids or prisoners.

The overall decoration of this parure is meant to suggest the various ethnic groups who populate the United States.

FLOWERED BROOCH AND BRACELET

The Du Jay firm began as an off-shoot of Hirsh & Leff, which had liquidated its business. In a long article on the costume jewelry industry that appeared in *Fortune* in 1946, Du Jay was named as one of the most successful costume jewelry manufacturers. The company was in operation in New York from 1934 through 1947. The costume jewelry produced by Du Jay (which rarely placed its trademark on its products) was the result of exceptional workmanship: the rhinestones in the pavé settings were always very small—about a millimeter in diameter; the enameling looked like dabs from an Expressionist painting; and the stones were always crystal.

The brooch illustrated here originated from a cast of rhodium-plated metal depicting a bunch of flowers. Two large roses, one in pavé-set rhinestones and the other in red glass stones, are complemented by a smaller daisy and buds in pavé-set rhinestones, alternating with leafy shoots set with yellow-orange navette-cut glass stones. The bracelet is rhodium-plated metal, with a central motif of flowers and leaves executed in rhinestone, violet and yellow-orange glass stones, and a red cabochon.

Manufacturer
Du Jay

Place and Date of Manufacture
United States, c. 1935

Materials and Techniques
Cast rhodium-plated metal, rhinestones, glass-paste stones

Mark
Du Jay (on the bracelet)

Provenance
Private collection, New York

Du Jay

BROOCHES IN THE SHAPE
OF BLACK NANNIES

**Place and Date
of Manufacture**
France or the United
States, 1935–40

**Materials and
Techniques**
Thermoplastic material,
probably polyester

Mark
None

Provenance
Costanza Fiani
Collection, Milan

As with the Wild West necklace and brooch on page 119, American designers often draw the themes of their jewelry from images of everyday life. These pins, in green, blue, brown, red, and black, are the result of the great wave of popularity engendered by the film *Gone with the Wind*, in which one of the main characters is Scarlet O'Hara's black nurse, Mammie.

PATRIOTIC BROOCHES IN RED BAKELITE

Place and Date of Manufacture
United States, 1935–40

Materials and Techniques
Molded Bakelite, plasticized wire, small celluloid chain, wood

Mark
None

Provenance
Private collection, New York

The heart-shaped brooch (bottom right) belongs with ornaments of a sentimental nature. In this case, it's a metaphor for the "shattered" love of the wives and girlfriends whose husbands and boyfriends volunteered to fight in Europe during the Second World War. At the same time, the heart signifies a bond with those who are far away. During the war years, the most popular brooches were the patriotic ones—flags, wings, the "V" for victory, or sailors' caps—because they were an expression of popular participation, especially on the part of women, in the war effort. The cherry brooch, on the other hand, reveals another type of ornament worn in difficult times. Brightly colored jewelry was meant to ward off worry, sadness, and anxiety about those who were far away. The brooch has red Bakelite fruit with green leaves furrowed with light veining. The cherry clusters hang from links attached to a celluloid chain which is fixed to an engraved wooden bar that acts as the fastener for the brooch.

LARGE FROG-SHAPED BROOCH

**Place and Date
of Manufacture**
United States, 1935–40

**Materials and
Techniques**
Bakelite, carved
wood, metal

Mark
None

Provenance
Private collection,
New York

The reason for Bakelite's great success in non-precious jewelry production is due to its low cost and malleability; moreover, it represents the aesthetics of the time.

The frog, whose etymological origin in Japanese means "that which returns," is in this sense a protector of travelers and wayfarers and was therefore adapted as an ornamental subject. Here, the exaggerated portrayal dates this brooch to the late 1930s. The frog, modeled in wood with gold-plated metal eyes, rests on a grassy mound made from both carved and smooth green Bakelite.

LARGE CONVERTIBLE BROOCH

This brooch is a telling example of why an anonymous object may yet be worthy of recognition for its beauty and its portrayal of the aesthetics of its time. This rhodium-plated metal brooch can be converted into two clips. It depicts four yellow glass-paste bellflowers veined in milky white, with simulated pearl pistils. The bellflowers fan out from a cluster of leaves in pavé-set and baguette rhinestones with a single glass pearl in the center. Using Venetian glass in costume jewelry is quite common in Europe—especially in France and Germany—and in the United States where Miriam Haskell was exceptional in endowing these glass components, whose traditions go back over centuries, with artistry and innovation.

Place and Date of Manufacture
United States, 1937

Materials and Techniques
Cast rhodium-plated metal, rhinestones, glass paste, simulated pearls

Mark
U.S. Pat. 2072080 (on the fastener that holds the two clips together)

Provenance
Private collection, New York

LARGE BROOCH IN THE SHAPE OF A VASE OF FLOWERS

Place and Date of Manufacture
United States, 1935–40

Materials and Techniques
Cast gold-plated and cold-enameled metal, glass stones, rhinestones.

Mark
None

Provenance
Private collection, Milan

The individual who created this brooch may not have been inspired by classic jewelry making, given that the black enamel vase and other colored enamels are not conventionally used for real jewelry. Because fine jewelry must last over time, it does not allow for the liberties of design typical of costume jewelry.

The vase in this brooch is convex and flattened. It is enameled in black and has a gold-plated band at the bottom covered with châton-cut rhinestones. The leaves are variously gold-plated metal, metal and rhinestone, or enameled in green. The flowers are rendered in blue enamel and red and blue glass stones, most of which are cabochons.

LARGE BROOCH IN THE SHAPE OF A COLEOPTERAN

This brooch in the shape of a coleopteran, a member of the beetle family, may have been created to celebrate this creature's beauty, which turns out to be extremely pleasing to the eye when interpreted so simply. But it may also derive from a widespread Latin American tradition which held that flying insects were the souls of the dead returning to visit the living.

The brooch originated from a copper casting, shaped to depict a flying insect whose body is formed by a large green oval crystal. The veining on the wings is highlighted by thin lines of black enamel. The attribution of this brooch to Eugene Joseff was determined by the color of the stone (green and topaz yellow were his preferred shades) and by its consciously *faux* impact.

Designer
Probably Eugene Joseff

Manufacturer
Probably Eugene Joseff

Place and Date of Manufacture
United States, late 1930s

Materials and Techniques
Cast copper, crystal

Mark
None

Provenance
Carolle Thibaut-Pomerantz Collection, Paris

COLLAR OF SMALL BEADS

Place and Date of Manufacture
Austria, c. 1928

Materials and Techniques
Frosted glass disks, small glass beads, aluminum caps

Mark
None

Provenance
Private collection, Vienna

This type of necklace, made from balls covered with small beads, was used in the very beautiful sautoirs designed by Felice Rix and Max Snischek and executed in crochet work for the Wiener Werkstätte. The exhibit "*Traum und Wirklichkeit, Wien 1870–1930*" ("Dream and Reality, Vienna 1830–1930"), held at the Historisches Museum der Stadt in Vienna in 1985 and its accompanying catalogue were dedicated to the work of the Wiener Werkstätte.

This collar is composed entirely of pairs of frosted blue glass disks alternating with small black-and-white beads. Each bead-covered ball is flanked with a small hollow cup in silver-plated metal stamped with incised lines.

MESHWORK COLLAR

The chain, originally designed as a functional component for supporting objects, charms, pendants, watches, or toiletries, is also used as a decorative element. For this reason, patterns for chains have increased in variety over time, and many kinds of processes, including mechanical, have been used to make them.

In this case, the chain serves two functions: it links together the decorative elements, and, it is itself an integral part of the design. The necklace is composed of several strands of small oval disks made from electric-blue enameled metal, arranged horizontally on the inner part of the necklace, and vertically to form the pendants. Five black-enameled triangles mark the center. The plates are connected and held in place by fine metal chains.

Place and Date of Manufacture
Austria, c. 1928

Materials and Techniques
Enameled metal plates, metal chain

Mark
None

Provenance
Private collection, Vienna

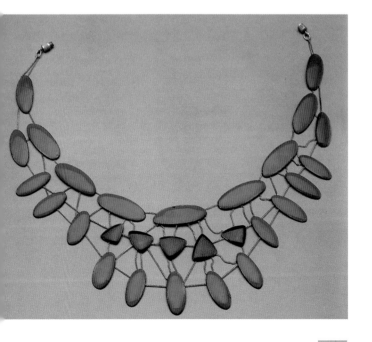

NECKTIE NECKLACE

**Place and Date
of Manufacture**
Venice, c. 1930

**Materials and
Techniques**
Venetian-glass seed
beads

Mark
None

Provenance
Private collection,
Milan

The tradition of weaving Venetian-glass seed beads is an extremely ancient one that spread to many different cultures, including the American Indians, as well as Africa and South America. In the 1920s and 1930s, Venetian beads were often used for small beaded bags and bandeaux, thin hair bands that held down the fashionable bobbed hair styles of the time.

This necklace can be regarded as derivative of the bandeau, revised and reinterpreted in order to add another touch of ambiguity to the boyish look of the time. The main part of the necklace, shaped like a necktie, is woven from red, orange, green, blue, and gray glass beads to create an overall floral pattern. The necktie beads are finished off with black glass paste balls and a graduated fringe of tassels.

RED AND BLACK GLASS-BEAD SAUTOIR

In this sautoir, numerous strands of small red and black glass beads are joined together by a red glass-carved wooden bead through which they pass and descend in cascades. The beads are joined at the back of the sautoir by another wooden bead, this one covered with horizontal rows of small black glass beads.

This necklace is noteworthy because of its innovative use of glass beads. In fact, the brilliance of the red and black glass beads is a perfect example of the color contrasts so typical of Art Deco: red for blood, life, and love; black for its opposite, night, death, and emptiness. Together, the two represent the positive and negative forces of nature.

Place and Date of Manufacture
Venice, c. 1930

Materials and Techniques
Venetian-glass seed beads, wood

Mark
None

Provenance
Private collection, Venice

MOLDED BAKELITE BROOCH

Place and Date of Manufacture
Italy, c. 1935

Materials and Techniques
Molded and partially painted Bakelite

Mark
None

Provenance
Veronica Guiduzzi Collection, Bologna

It is interesting to note how a simple object made from inexpensive materials, such as this one, can succeed in evoking a complicated social and political situation: Mussolini (the heavy-set mastiff) with his angry expression is trying to take Ethiopia (the bone) away from Haile Sellassie (the poor, thin, bony dog) who does not want to yield to the force of his adversary. This is an anonymous artisan's unique interpretation of Mussolini's "triumphant" conquest of Ethiopia. The brooch is molded Bakelite, partially painted in shades of ocher, red, and black, and depicts two stylized dogs on a green rectangular base fighting over a bone.

CAMEL AND DUNES BUCKLE

As has already been mentioned, few pieces of Italian period costume jewelry can be found either in the antiques trade or displayed in applied arts museums. This makes it hard to learn much about Italian jewelry productions. However, there does exist a variety of buckles, which were worn by women who had their dresses made by tailors. Through the fifties, this kind of woman always wore real jewelry and the only nonprecious accessories she willingly accepted were buckles and buttons, whose eccentricities she forgave as long as they could personalize her outfit.

This buckle is certainly not a conventional specimen. Made from open-work, gold-plated, stamped metal with a rectangular line, it depicts an Egyptian landscape of dunes and palm trees with a camel in the center. The exotic inspiration for the choice of theme may suggest a historical reference to the then recent Italian colonization of Libya and conquest of Ethiopia.

Place and Date of Manufacture
Italy, late 1930s

Materials and Techniques
Stamped gold-plated metal

Mark
None

Provenance
Donatella Stranier Collection, Bologna

CROSS-SHAPED BROOCH WITH SIMULATED TOPAZES

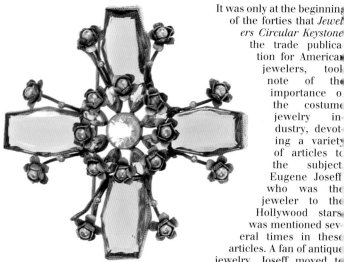

It was only at the beginning of the forties that *Jewelers Circular Keystone* the trade publication for American jewelers, took note of the importance of the costume jewelry industry, devoting a variety of articles to the subject. Eugene Joseff who was the jeweler to the Hollywood stars was mentioned several times in these articles. A fan of antique jewelry, Joseff moved to Hollywood in 1929 and, over the course of a few years, established himself as the preeminent jeweler of the film industry, specializing in jewelry for period films and epics such as *Gone with the Wind* (1939).

This brooch, in stamped gold-plated metal in the shape of a cross, is formed of four geometrically shaped, faceted crystal stones in simulated topaz. A wreath of gold-plated metal flowers with navettes of orange stones centered with a brilliant-cut rhinestone radiate out from the cross.

Designer
Eugene Joseff

Manufacturer
Eugene Joseff

Place and Date of Manufacture
Los Angeles, c. 1940

Materials and Techniques
Stamped gold-plated metal, faceted stones

Mark
Joseff Hollywood

Provenance
Private collection

JOSEFF
HOLLYWOOD

BROOCH IN THE SHAPE OF AN ANEMONE

Stamped gold-plated metal distinguishes this stylized anemone brooch, with its smooth, overlapping petals arranged in a cuplike shape, spherical pistil, and stem adorned with two notched leaves.

Gold came back into fashion in the forties as a reaction, in part, to the white jewelry that had been in vogue in the thirties. Furthermore, the white metals that had been used were now conscripted for military purposes. This brooch, though it is a significant example of forties style, is atypical of jewelry signed with the name Sandor.

SANDOR

Manufacturer
Sandor

Place and Date of Manufacture
United States, early 1940s

Materials and Techniques
Stamped gold-plated metal

Mark
Sandor

Provenance
Costanza Fiani Collection, Milan

This firm, which was in business from the end of the thirties to the mid-seventies, was best known for the excellence of its cold-enameled costume jewelry, in pastel colors inset with materials such as mother-of-pearl or glass paste simulating semiprecious stones.

CONVERTIBLE
"DUETTE" BROOCH

Coro DUETTE

Designer
Adolph Katz

Manufacturer
Cohn & Rosenberger

**Place and Date
of Manufacture**
United States, c. 1940

**Materials and
Techniques**
Cast gold-plated and
partially enameled sil-
ver, faceted glass stones

Mark
Coro Duette (on both the
fastener and the clips)

Provenance
"Epoque" Collection,
Bologna

Cohn & Rosenberger, the largest American manufacturer of costume jewelry, employing more than eight thousand workers in 1946, would probably not have become so famous were it not for the "duette" pin—twin clips that could be worn either individually or specially fastened to make a single brooch. The device for holding the two clips together was patented in 1930 by Gaston Candas, a Parisian who had moved to the United States. Shortly thereafter, Cohn & Rosenberger acquired the rights to the patent and launched the duette on the fashion jewelry market in a wide variety of designs.

Each of the clips that make up this brooch depicts a leafy branch. When joined together, the shoots form a gold-plated, asymmetrical oval motif with the leaves highlighted by green enameling. The flowers are two orangeish faceted stones, simulating topaz, encircled with pavé-set rhinestone corollas.

FILIGREED METAL BROOCH

In the panorama of American costume jewelry manufacturers, Hobé is known as a producer of luxury items—jewelry with an antique flavor, rich with extremely brilliant crystals connected by filigreed motifs, and wrought with the skill and proficiency of a master craftsman. During the forties, Hobé jewels were promoted by the most beloved stars with the catchy slogan "Jewels of Legendary Splendor."

Constructed in filigreed gold-plated metal, this brooch is in three parts: a quadrangular shape for the center and two semicircles, one at either side. The main design, with alternating rhinestones and blue glass cabochons, has a double frame, braided thin spirals of gold-plated metal, and tapered and faceted blue glass baguettes. The semicircles have three rhinestones arranged in a trefoil with a small blue cabochon in the middle, surrounded by a band of tapered blue baguettes with a single rhinestone mounted at the outermost point.

Manufacturer
Hobé

Place and Date of Manufacture
United States, c. 1940

Materials and Techniques
Filigree metal, glass stones

Mark
Hobé

Provenance
Private collection, New York

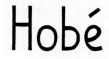

BROOCH IN THE SHAPE OF
A BOUQUET OF FLOWERS

Designer
Alfred Philippe

Manufacturer
Trifari, Krussman
& Fishel

**Place and Date
of Manufacture**
United States,
early 1940s

**Materials and
Techniques**
Cast rhodium-plated
and enameled metal,
rhinestones

Mark
Trifari

Provenance
Private collection,
New York

This bouquet brooch, colored with enamel and
created at the beginning of the forties by Alfred
Philippe for Trifari, revives a technique beloved
of American jewelry makers; especially Tiffany,
who exhibited its own fire-enameled brooches
shaped like orchids at the International Exhibit in Paris in 1889. The fire-enameling technique was simplified for costume jewelry by
using synthetic cold enamel, which required
less exacting craftsmanship and was therefore
less costly.

Rhodium-plated metal casting was used to
create this delicate bunch of flowers. The flower
petals, decorated with enamel in muted shades
of pink, lilac, and ivory, are outlined by slender
bands of pavé-set rhinestones. The green-enam-
eled stems and leaves, trimmed with both pavé-
set and individually mounted rhinestones, are
tied by a delicate rhinestone bow.

BROOCH WITH
FRUITED STALKS

The line of this brooch suggests the art of wrought ironwork as a likely source of inspiration; in particular furniture, with explicit references to the grips and plates on chests of drawers and trunks. The choice of exuberant images for the brooch recalls the world of film and theater, both of which influenced American jewelry fashions, real and costume, especially so in the thirties and forties. In this instance, the fruit-adorned bough suggests the headdresses worn by Carmen Miranda as well as Josephine Baker's stage costume.

The main structure of the brooch derives from a metal casting of a plant shoot in pavé-set rhinestones. The rhinestone leaves alternate with glass pastes stamped in the shape of fruits, some engraved and dyed in shades of red, green, and yellow. In the center and at the tips of the bough are two bands of châton-cut rhinestones.

Place and Date of Manufacture
United States, c. 1940

Materials and Techniques
Cast rhodium-plated metal, stamped glass paste, rhinestones

Mark
None

Provenance
"Epoque" Collection, Bologna

GOLD-PLATED METAL AND RHINESTONE BROOCHES

Designer
1. Elvira De Rosa

Manufacturer
1. Ralph De Rosa, Inc.
2. Fred A. Block, Inc.

Place and Date of Manufacture
1. New York, c. 1940
2. Chicago, c. 1940

Materials and Techniques
Cast gold-plated and enameled metal, glass stones, rhinestones, simulated pearls

Mark
1. De Rosa
2. Fred A. Block Jewelry

Provenance
1. Private collection, Bologna
2. Carolle Thibaut-Pomerantz Collection, Paris

1

De Rosa, a firm made up of three women of Italian descent (Elvira, the designer, Virginia, the president, and Theresa) worked out of New York from 1933 to 1955. De Rosa's creations are characterized by exaggerated bows, abundant spirals, and bouquets overflowing with pearls and colored crystals. They tend to be fanciful, but stylistically they are perfectly coherent, harmonious, and elegant.

Fred A. Block's costume jewelry, enameled and with the large stones that are traditionally used by Chicago jewelry manufacturers Eisenberg and Staret, have a strong visual impact.

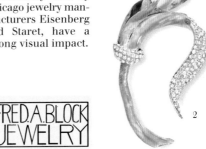

2

LARGE BOW-SHAPED PIN

Frank A. J. Pennino, a company that specialized in the manufacturing of precious jewelry, was founded in New York in 1926. In 1932 the company became Pennino Bros. Under the management of Oreste Pennino, the company branched out and began to produce objects made in gold-plated metal. This brooch is typical of Pennino's production, which specialized in naturalistic objects in bright colors with rounded, sinuous shapes such as bows or bunches of flowers. Only rarely did the jewelry focus on a figurative subject, which were almost always drawn from Italian traditions such as Pinocchio or Pulcinella.

Cast in gold-plated silver, this brooch was molded in the shape of a bow formed of four smooth ribbons held together in the center by ten four-petaled flowers made of faceted green glass stones. Each flower has a rhinestone pistil.

Manufacturer
Pennino Bros.

Place and Date of Manufacture
United States, c. 1940

Materials and Techniques
Cast gold-plated metal, glass stones

Mark
Pennino

Provenance
Private collection, Milan

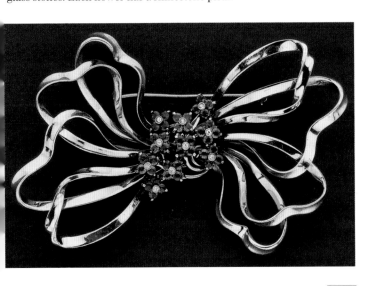

CLIP WITH A CLUSTER
OF WALNUTS

Designer
Frank Hess

Manufacturer
Miriam Haskell Jewels

**Place and Date
of Manufacture**
New York, c. 1940

**Materials and
Techniques**
Wood, gold-plated
metallic components,
plastic tube

Mark
None

Provenance
Collezione Lo Scrigno
del Tempo, Avellino,
Italy

In 1934, a Miami daily newspaper announced a lecture to be given by Miriam Haskell as follows: "A New York designer of ultra-modern jewelry that has the charm of magical antique family jewels, even though they are made from ordinary, everyday materials." This pin is indicative of the time when the Miriam Haskell company, like so many other American firms, was forced to give up using the glass beads and stones imported from Czechoslovakia, France, and Venice that had marked her creations from the beginning. She then adapted natural and synthetic materials of indigenous origin.

This unusual clip depicts a cluster of walnuts in carved wood suspended on small gold-plated chains which are attached to a mount that also serves as a support for the two large gold-plated leaves. Small beads connect the nuts, and the gold-plated ends are in the shape of rosettes.

MOTHER-OF-PEARL NECKLACE

In the period jewelry market, the most well-known and sought-after objects made by Miriam Haskell are her rosy-toned baroque pearls. This appeal probably has its origins in the traditional rope of pearls that has consistently come back into popularity over the centuries as one of the most beloved ornaments. Considering the wide variety of Haskell jewelry, perhaps one naturally chooses pearls by virtue of their long-standing popularity. In fact, Haskell's pearl jewelry should be recognized for its unprecedented variety and refined finishing touches that succeed in giving a very personal touch to a material that is generally mounted in a repetitive style. It is unconventional ornaments like this necklace that best reveal the essential Haskell, a woman who loved nature and art and who frequented museums and antique auctions.

The necklace is a single strand of mother-of-pearl alternated with baroque pearls fashioned from dark-gray glass and connected by burnished metal fittings. The pendant is a trilobate plant design in mother-of-pearl with fruit in the middle, gray baroque pearls, and four metal leaves, two of them chased with veins and two covered in small gray glass beads. The hexagonal clasp is stamped filigree metal with a circle of small beads and, in the center of the circle, a small dark-gray glass pearl mounted on the filigree.

Designer
Frank Hess

Manufacturer
Miriam Haskell Jewels

Place and Date of Manufacture
New York, c. 1940

Materials and Techniques
Mother-of-pearl beads and components, glass baroque pearls, metal clasp and fittings

Mark
Miriam Haskell

Provenance
Private collection, Milan

145

BROOCH OF YELLOW AND WHITE FLOWERS

Designer
Frank Hess

Manufacturer
Miriam Haskell Jewels

Place and Date
of Manufacture
New York, c. 1940

Materials and
Techniques
Glass paste, hollow
small tubes and
balls, stamped-glass
components, gold-
plated metal rivets

Mark
None

Provenance
Private collection,
Milan

In her work, Miriam Haskell has always gone against the current. When she opened a small shop in the Mc-Alpin Hotel in New York, the trait that distinguished her jewelry was its handcraftsmanship at a time when all the other manufacturers were preoccupied with perfecting machines capable of making ever-increasing numbers of pieces at lower costs.

In 1930, when white jewelry in geometric shapes was in vogue, Haskell dedicated herself exclusively to creating costume jewelry made from colored glass, destined for the woman who liked bright styles and who spent her leisure time vacationing in Miami or Biarritz. In 1943 the average cost of a costume jewelry bracelet was one dollar. But if it was a Haskell bracelet the average cost rose to forty-three dollars. The high cost was justified by the extensive handwork required for each object, as was the case with this brooch which depicts three flowers "sewn" and fastened with metallic thread to a plastic mount.

The corolla is fashioned from small looped tubes of white glass paste that are slipped onto a gallery of stamped metal shaped like a flower and sewn in place. The flower pistils are made from yellow glass-paste balls held in place by gold-plated metal rivets. Four large leaves in stamped green glass complete the brooch.

BROOCH IN THE SHAPE OF A STEM OF FLOWERS

Eisenberg costume jewelry is the quintessential American bauble: decidedly fake, in out-of-the-ordinary proportions, with stones that are much too big to be real. The Chicago firm Eisenberg & Sons has been in business since 1914. Though the firm still produces costume jewelry, their glory years ran from the thirties until just after the Second World War. The success of Eisenberg jewelry probably inspired other entrepreneurs with a desire to enter the costume jewelry field, which was a growth industry in those years. Thus, Staret Jewelry was founded in 1941, manufacturing jewelry similar to that made by Eisenberg. Around 1940, Fred A. Block, a clothing manufacturer, expanded into costume jewelry production.

This brooch was cast in white metal molded to represent a branch culminating in two flowers made from two large faceted stones of clear crystal. The stem is studded with eleven smaller buds in rhinestone alternated with leaves, four enameled in green and three with smaller pavé-set rhinestones.

Manufacturer
Eisenberg & Sons

Place and Date of Manufacture
Chicago, c. 1940

Materials and Techniques
Partially enameled cast white metal, faceted crystal stones, rhinestones

Mark
Eisenberg Original

Provenance
Bersia Antichità Collection, Milan

BROOCH IN THE SHAPE OF A FISH

Manufacturer
Attributed to Marcel Boucher

Place and Date of Manufacture
United States, late 1940s

Materials and Techniques
Gold-plated and rhodium-plated cast metal, faceted stone, rhinestones

Mark
None

Provenance
Private collection, New York

This fantasy fish, which can be dated to the forties because of its rosy gold-plating (yellow was used in the following years), seems to anticipate the fanciful creatures that would come into fashion in the fifties. These creatures were to be masterfully interpreted in jewelry by Fulco di Verdura and Jean Schlumberger. The brooch can be attributed to Marcel Boucher because of its style and its unconventional subject, which is rendered with elegance and enriched with a stone whose intense blue color evokes tropical seas and clear skies. This brooch was perfect for embellishing the severe, square jackets of the new kind of woman who was just coming onto the scene in those years: the career woman.

This brooch is a metal casting, molded to depict the fish, whose body has been gold-plated and engraved in order to define its scales; in the mouth of the fish is a large blue, navette-cut glass stone. The fins and tail are adorned with small pavé-set rhinestones.

SIMULATED TOPAZ
BRACELET AND BROOCH

The Ciner Manufacturing Co. was founded in 1892 by Emanuel Ciner, the grandfather of the current owner, Pat Hill. The daughter of Irvin Ciner, she married David Hill who became president of Ciner in 1979 after his father-in-law retired. Up until 1930 the firm manufactured real jewelry, but subsequently turned to the production of costume jewelry, which shows strong traces of its heritage.

In fact, Ciner costume jewels are executed using the same techniques used for making real jewelry, as well as similar subjects and styles. Ciner only uses stones with natural colors and gilding that is very similar in appearance to 18 carat gold; each stone and rhinestone is mounted with great care. This matching bracelet and brooch are a good example of traditional techniques married to contemporary shapes and styles. The bracelet is a rigid band of smooth, gold-plated metal inset with five rows of small glass stones. The central portion is composed of a semicircle of ribbed, gold-plated metal adorned by six

rows of orange-yellow oval glass stones imitating topaz, which was made popular in those years by the Duchess of Windsor, who was partial to this stone.

The brooch has the same design as the central portion of the bracelet.

Manufacturer
Ciner Manufacturing Co.

Place and Date of Manufacture
New York, c. 1940

Materials and Techniques
Cast gold-plated metal, faceted stones

Mark
Ciner

Provenance
Private collection

CRYSTAL
LINK BRACELET

**Place and Date
of Manufacture**
France, early 1940s

**Materials and
Techniques**
Gold-plated metal,
transparent crystal,
imitation stone in
faceted oval-cut red
glass

Mark
None

Provenance
Private collection

This hinged link bracelet is composed of squares of transparent crystal enclosed in a thin frame of gold-plated metal with an oval-shaped medallion, also in crystal, in the center. A faceted red crystal stone, simulating a ruby, is mounted in a pronged setting on the medallion.

Few pieces of jewelry so clearly mark the passage from one style to the next as does this bracelet. The typical pairing of diamonds and platinum in thirties jewelry (which became rhinestones and rhodium-plated metal in costume jewelry) is partially represented by the clear crystal used in this bracelet. The delicate gold-plated metal acts as a foil to the crystal. After the popularity of the white jewelry of the preceding era, the gold color will hold sway throughout the forties. The gold is reinforced and enhanced by the bright-red central stone, which makes the combination of color and noncolor even more dramatic.

INCISED PLASTIC BROOCHES
WITH RHINESTONES

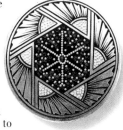

Brooches of this type were produced in Oyonnax, a small mountain town in the French Jura, a town which over the course of the nineteenth century miraculously succeeded in becoming a small industrial city, to the point that it now has a population of almost 25,000 people involved in the manufacturing of combs. These combs were first made from wood, then horn, and beginning in 1880, from celluloid. Around the 1920s, in reaction to short hair, the manufacturers began to produce other articles, especially costume jewels, buckles, and buttons, but also eyeglass frames, boxes, lamps, and toys, all made from plastics.

These brooches were produced during the Second World War, another difficult moment for industry in Oyonnax. (Business picked up after the war and subsequently entered into a new period of expansion. Today, more than 700 firms are devoted to manufacturing a variety of items made from plastics.) Circular brooches, like those shown here, were executed in black acetate, silver-plated, and colored in a variety of designs using the electrotyping process; engraving emphasized the edges of the decorations. Further embellishments were obtained on the two brooches at the top of the page and on the one in the middle by cold-setting, respectively, red, clear, and orange rhinestones and by manually inserting small tin findings that call to mind fine granules.

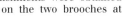

Place and Date of Manufacture
Oyonnax (France), 1939–45

Materials and Techniques
Handworked acetate, rhinestones, small tin findings

Mark
None

Provenance
Antichità De Giovanni Collection, Milan

GOLD-PLATED ACETATE
BROOCHES AND PENDANT

Manufacturer
Probably Auguste
Bonaz for the leaf
brooch at top (unknown
for the other brooches
and pendant)

**Place and Date
of Manufacture**
Oyonnax (France),
1939–45

**Materials and
Techniques**
Gold-plated acetate,
using an electrotyping
process; gold leaf over
plastic for the leaf at
the top

Mark
None

Provenance
Private collection

Each of the three
brooches depicts a
leaf, the pendant a
branch with fruit.
These models, to-
gether with those on
the previous page,
give a good indication
of the types of plastic
ornaments produced
in Oyonnax. This city
is the home of the Musée du Peigne et des
Matières Plastiques, with its collection of extremely interesting objects (combs, plates,
centerpieces, and other decorative items) that
are in large part unpublished. Naturally, the
museum stresses the history of the comb, the
object that stimulated the development of a
rural mountain village into a small industrial
city. The first document in the city archives
that mentions "comb makers" goes back to
1667, when farmers turned to this activity during the winter months. As early as the begin-

ning of the nineteenth
century, "fashionable
combs" are men-
tioned. From then on,
the comb industry
prospered and ex-
ported its products to
all of Europe.

COLLAR WITH
SIMULATED TOPAZES

The sensation caused by the marriage of King Edward VIII of England to Wallis Simpson, a commoner and a divorcée, also had repercussions for the history of jewels and costume jewelry. Gems that up until that time had been considered to be of little value, when worn by her, enjoyed their brief moment of glory. Such was the case of topaz which was widely used in the forties for both jewelry and fashion ornaments.

This collar necklace is fashioned from transparent crystal rings, each of which is connected to its neighbors by three rings of gold-plated metal. The centerpiece of the necklace is made up of seven faceted drop pendants in various shades of yellow glass imitating topaz. Small glass balls, also simulating topaz, are interspersed among the pendant drops.

Place and Date of Manufacture
France or the United States, early 1940s

Materials and Techniques
Glass or gold-plated metal rings, faceted glass stones, glass balls

Mark
None

Provenance
Carolle Thibaut-Pomerantz Collection, Paris

BROOCH IN THE
SHAPE OF AN IRIS

Manufacturer
Unidentified

Place and Date of Manufacture
Probably Paris, late 1940s

Materials and Techniques
Stamped metal, resin

Mark
Félix (on the stem),
Deposé (on the clasp)

Provenance
Private collection, Paris

This brooch is emblematic of the difficulty involved in determining the paternity of a particular object, even when one has information on which to base an attribution. The style of the brooch is indicative of the forties. In fact, the theme of the iris plucked at the height of its glory was picked up from Art Nouveau, but here it is treated from the viewpoint of the forties, an era that exaggerated its subjects and endowed then with greater incisiveness and power. The mark "Félix" does not ring a bell with the exception of a dressmaker's establishment called Félix, in operation in Paris in the second half of the nineteenth century, where Jeanne Lanvin worked at the beginning of her successful career as a couturier. It is not improbable that this same house also produced costume jewelry, but we can't confirm this with any degree of certainty.

This brooch is stamped gold-plated metal. The structure was executed in metal and the petals in a deep-rose granular resin.

Félix

COLLAR WITH SIMULATED PEARLS AND GREEN STONES

The back part of this necklace is made up of two rounds of glass simulated pearls covered by a large green glass-paste cabochon stone, surrounded by a crown of smaller simulated pearls. In front, the pearls are part of three round clusters, called *voluptés* by Louis Rousselet. They are formed on a base made from silver-plated wire bent into the shape of a six-petalled corolla, to which pearls and green glass petals and stones, shaped like drops or balls, simulated pearls, and small beads are attached.

This necklace, with its classic festooned shape, is well-suited to the fashions that followed Christian Dior's New Look. At that time, having regained her femininity, a woman could allow herself to wear tasteful accessories that were at the same time elegantly "voluptuous," as their creator chose to call them.

Designer
Louis Rousselet

Manufacturer
Louis Rousselet

Place and Date of Manufacture
France, 1948

Materials and Techniques
Glass simulated pearls, glass-paste stones, silver-plated metal components

Mark
Made in France

Provenance
Private collection

L.R

PAINTED GALALITH BUCKLES

Place and Date of Manufacture
Italy, late 1930s

Materials and Techniques
Handworked, partially painted galalith; gold-plated metal components

Mark
None

Provenance
Costanza Fiani Collection, Milan

In times of famine, luxury goods and frivolities are the first things to be sacrificed. People also tend to economize on fashions, and so in the forties skirts became shorter and waistlines became tighter. Loose gathers at the hips and below the bustline were all that remained to soften the lines of the body. Therefore, the belt became the fundamental element of an outfit, and a buckle was the only touch of coquetry that an elegant woman allowed herself.

The buckle at the lower right is black galalith in a rectangular shape with rounded corners, adorned with ten appliquéd small dogs also made from galalith in a variety of colors: blue, yellow, red, aquamarine, and white. The buckle at the lower left, made of aquamarine galalith, bears the phrase which also produces its shape, "*penso sempre a te*" ("I'm always thinking about you"). The buckle directly below is the most unusual of the three. It is made of two sections of ivory galalith with looped decorations painted to look like they were sewn together. The loops are attached to the buckle by rivets finished with small gold-plated balls.

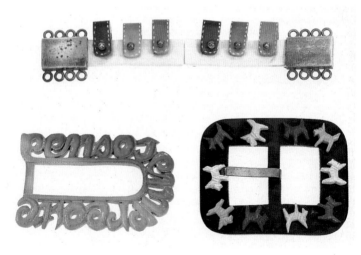

BROOCH IN THE SHAPE OF A NEST

Place and Date of Manufacture
Italy, late 1930s or early 1940s

Materials and Techniques
Painted wood, raffia, coral, wire

Mark
None

Provenance
Costanza Fiani Colection, Milan

Despite the war and fascism, news about Hollywood film stars also reached Italy. But the life of these stars was unattainable for people who were suffering. Carmen Miranda's headdresses and costumes, in which exotic fruits gave rise to elaborate, vivacious shapes, certainly struck the fancy of common people in Italy as elsewhere. But Rome was not Hollywood and Italians had to make do with their sense of imagination and the humble materials at their disposal—wood, cork, coral, shells, raffia, and straw. They created fantastic objects with these materials; objects that were simple, modern, full of color, and different from anything that had been seen in the past. These ornaments that were so different from American jewelry—glittering, opulent, and designed to change film stars into goddesses—had an immediate success abroad, where the scarcity of materials was mistakenly seen as a desire for simplicity. This brooch is composed of overlapping balls of natural wood, painted in shades of olive green. Twigs of red coral are connected by thin wire to the wood ball.

LARGE BROOCH IN THE SHAPE
OF A QUESTION MARK

Designer
Federico Pallavicini

Manufacturer
Giuliano Fratti

**Place and Date
of Manufacture**
Italy, 1942

**Materials and
Techniques**
Wire, thin cord, string,
simulated pearls, glass
balls, crystal stones

Mark
None

Provenance
Civiche Raccolte d'Arte
Applicata, Milan

This brooch was published in the October 1942 issue of *Bellezza* at a time when Giuliano Fratti had for years been the most famous *parurier* in Italy. The first reviews of his work date back to 1933, when his belts for Tizzini were noticed at the 14th Milan Fair. In 1940, he began to issue his own costume jewelry and buttons. Because Fratti specialized in replicas of French jewelry, it is no surprise that this brooch was designed not by him, but by a professional designer.

The brooch is shaped like a feather composed of a stem and an incomplete spiral made of stiff wire. The stem, covered with thin gilded cord alternating with blue and pink threads, is attached to the spiral by a corolla adorned with a semicircle of simulated pearls, red glass beads, and drop-shaped stones made from green crystal.

At the top, the spiral, also wrapped in thin gilded cord but with black threads, is surmounted by simulated pearls, red glass stones, and bands of blue thread. The threads support gilded cord tassels that are arranged like a halo along the profile of the spiral.

LARGE BROOCH IN THE SHAPE OF A BUNCH OF GRAPES

During the period of autarchy, Italian designers had to resort to natural materials that were available locally, as is demonstrated by their use of wood, coral, raffia, and grape seeds. Costume jewels that resulted from well-chosen processing and coloring of these humble materials were original and cheerful. They were also a way to drive away the demons of fear and sorrow that beset people during the war. These jewels were also sufficiently elegant and different that by the beginning of the forties Giuliano Fratti was able to successfully export this type of jewelry to the United States.

This brooch is shaped like a bunch of grapes. Each grape is a wooden ball painted in shades of fuchsia and attached to the base of the brooch by a rivet with a large gold-plated metal head. A bunch of grapes has always been a favorite subject for jewelry because it is a symbol of abundance and a sign of good luck.

Place and Date of Manufacture
Italy, c. 1940

Materials and Techniques
Painted wood, stamped gold-plated metal

Mark
None

Provenance
Costanza Fiani Collection, Milan

PAIRS OF GEOMETRIC CLIPS

Manufacturer
Calderoni Gioielli

**Place and Date
of Manufacture**
Milan, 1942–46

**Materials and
Techniques**
Handworked gold-
plated or silver-plated
metal

Mark
None

Provenance
Ornella Archives, Milan

Calderoni Gioielli, one of the most important firms in Italy, is a manufacturer and distributor of jewelry and silver objects. From 1942 to 1946, because of the war, the firm changed its production line in order to keep the company's employees on the the payroll. Due to a lack of gold, Calderoni turned to manufacturing nonprecious ornaments whose styles show the graceful, expert hand of the professional jeweler.

These four pairs of clips—in silver-plated or gold-plated metal, cut and turned by hand—are shaped to depict smooth, curling ribbons with simple, harmonious lines. The preservation of this material—low in intrinsic value, but important as a historical document—is due to the sensitivity of Piera Barni Albani, the proprietor of Ornella, a manufacturer of costume jewelry. When she set up her own business in 1946, Albani took over the unsold stock of Gi. Vi. Emme, for whom these metal trinkets had been produced. Partial credit also goes to her daughter Maria Vittoria Albani, who succeeded her mother and has continued to preserve these objects.

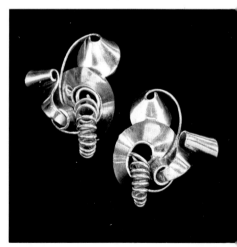

SERIES OF THREE FIGURATIVE BROOCHES

These brooches represent the first phase of Ornella jewelry production. When Ornella was first in business, the firm entrusted the designs for the jewelry it intended to produce to a professional designer whose full name has been lost. Of the multitude of designs created by this individual that are still in existence, only one bears a signature, which we have deciphered as "Cannelli Bizzani."

In the bellflower brooch below, the flower rests amid three green-painted lanceolate leaves. The base of the leaves are gathered around a red-painted berry, and an alert squirrel leans against one of the leaves.

The brooch at upper right is a casting of tricolor gold-plated metal depicting a rabbit sitting on a branch and playing a trumpet. The eyes are glass paste. Below, is a casting of tricolor gold-plated metal depicting a gazelle beside a tree. The eyes are cabochon-cut glass paste. The subjects of both brooches are rendered in a very realistic fashion, with great attention to detail.

Designer
Cannelli Bizzani

Manufacturer
Ditta Ornella

Place and Date of Manufacture
Milan, 1948–50

Materials and Techniques
Partially enameled and gold-plated cast metal, glass paste

Mark
None

Provenance
Ornella Archives, Milan

CORAL AND SIMULATED
LAPIS LAZULI CHOKER

Designer
Lyda Coppola

Manufacturer
Coppola & Toppo for
Elsa Schiaparelli

**Place and Date
of Manufacture**
Italy, 1949

Mark
Made in Italy

Provenance
Private collection,
Milan

A very similar necklace with the same circular
design of small branches of coral was published
in French *Vogue* in March of 1949. Another one,
again very like this model, appeared on the
cover of American *Vogue* in November 1949.

Considering the bleak years immediately
after the war, it would seem that these objects,
so extraordinary in their unconventional use
of crystal, enjoyed a success that remained un-
equaled by all other Italian makers, often extremely famous at home, but practically unknown abroad.

The necklace is two strands of blue glass-
paste beads, imitating lapis lazuli, placed
between two lateral half-moon-shaped coral
branches "sewn" on a base made of a sheet of
brass and an overhanging gold-plated gallery.

The rose-shaped clasp is gold plate set
with coral beads and with a blue glass-paste
bead in the center.

NECKLACE
WITH CAMEO

This necklace, published in the first issue of *Bellezza* in January 1949, reveals how diligently the Italian fashion press signaled new trends. In fact, in that year Coppola & Toppo, a group created by Lyda Coppola, had only been in business for a few months, but they already counted among their clients important French firms like Schiaparelli, Jacques Fath, Piquet, and Molineux. All this at a time when the French fashion industry was known to be notoriously lacking in generosity over creations from places other than Paris. Coppola & Toppo created costume jewelry made entirely by hand and marked "Miky," the name of Lyda Coppola's dog.

This necklace is three strands of simulated pearls separated by small glass beads. In the center of the clasp, an antique tortoise-shell cameo, depicting a woman's head, is enclosed inside an oval frame made up of a circlet of pearls. Three pendants, each composed of five pearls, hang from the cameo. This necklace is typical of Molineux's classic, timeless style.

Designer
Lyda Coppola

Manufacturer
Coppola & Toppo
for Molineux, Paris

Place and Date of Manufacture
Milan, 1949

Materials and Techniques
Glass simulated pearls and small beads, antique tortoise-shell cameo mounted on a brass medallion

Mark
Miky

Provenance
Private collection, Milan

LARGE BROOCH WITH A SIMULATED TOPAZ

Manufacturer
Theodor Fahrner

Place and Date of Manufacture
Pforzheim (Germany), c. 1936

Materials and Techniques
Granulated and filigreed silver, topaz, marcasite

Mark
TF (crossed)

Provenance
Private collection

This large gold-plated silver brooch, worked in a technique called "granulation," depicts two soft leaves, decorated with filigreed spirals and marked with marcasite veins down the middle. In the center of the brooch, the leaves enfold a large oval-cut topaz.

Beginning in 1932 when Fahrner created their filigree jewelry collection, granulated embellishments and filigree—made by soldering twisted wire onto the surface of a piece of jewelry—have been the hallmarks of the firm's work. This 1932 collection, launched by Gustav Braendle who had taken over the firm after Theodor Fahrner's death, was one of the last ones to enjoy great success and widespread attention before the outbreak of the Second World War. The war naturally forced a reduction in jewelry production.

LARGE BROOCH WITH LEAVES AND FRUIT

The silverwork tradition in the Nordic countries goes back a very long way, but it reached the height of its creativity and international reputation with the mass-produced jewelry manufactured by Georg Jensen in Copenhagen.

The most important factor for the industry at the beginning of the Second World War was the disappearance of decorative materials other than metals, caused by Sweden's isolation from the rest of Europe. As a result, Swedish manufacturers had to rely on metal. As never before or after this time, ornaments seemed naked: the functionalism and rationalism of the twenties and thirties had deprived jewelry of its frills. This silver brooch is fashioned in the shape of a branch with four leaves surrounding an imagined fruit. The two central leaves are finely engraved in order to bring out the veins of the leaves.

Manufacturer
Unidentified

Place and Date of Manufacture
Sweden, late 1940s

Materials and Techniques
Stamped silver

Mark
Engel

Provenance
Private collection

BROOCH WITH MADREPORE

Manufacturer
Simone Dumas,
probably for Lola
Prusac

**Place and Date
of Manufacture**
France, early 1950s

**Materials and
Techniques**
Madrepore skeleton,
silver-plated metal
base, glass-paste
beads and spacers

Mark
None

Provenance
Private collection

Simone Dumas was an artisan in business
through the end of the sixties who worked
primarily for Lola Prusac. Her specialty was
assembling and finishing jewelry designed
by stylists and *paruriers*. The great skill that
marked her work is well recognized.

This brooch is the fruit of an assemblage of
traditional materials combined with a madrepore skeleton, a rather unusual jewelry component. The madrepore, mounted on a silver-
plated metal base, has a rounded icy-white
shape with a hole in the middle and a great
many slender spicules radiating outwards. Also
attached to the base are "branches" formed of
two flattened beads of transparent glass with
milky glass inclusions. A white glass spacer
separates the two beads. The branches are finished off with a coral-colored glass spacer.

LARGE FLOWER SCARF PIN

This pin is attributed to Jacques Fath because the elderly woman who owned it remembered having purchased it in his boutique. In addition, the crystals used in the brooch are in shades of gray, the dressmaker's favorite color for his accessories in the late forties and early fifties. The crystals also recall the work of other designers. Fath was partial to Coppola & Toppo, Gripoix, and Scemama. Although this pin is similar to those made by Lyda Coppola around this time, it cannot be attributed to her with absolute certainty.

This brooch depicts a flower whose petals are formed of iridescent gray crystals and small Venetian glass beads. The outline of the petals and the center of the corolla are set off by charcoal gray crystals sewn on a perforated metallic support.

Manufacturer
Unknown, probably for Jacques Fath

Place and Date of Manufacture
France, early 1950s

Materials and Techniques
Crystals, metallic gallery

Mark
Deposé

Provenance
Private collection

COLLAR NECKLACE

Designer
Madeleine Rivière

Manufacturer
Madeleine Rivière

Place and Date of Manufacture
Paris, late 1940s
or early 1950s

Materials and Techniques
Various sizes of simulated pearls, metallic links and components, glass-paste balls

Mark
France

Provenance
Private collection

The Societé Madeleine Rivière, specializing in the manufacture of costume jewelry, was founded around 1930 and made a name for itself on the French market thanks to the ingenuity of Madame Rivière herself. The firm was sold to Madame Gallet in 1950, who further expanded the company, producing jewelry for Dior, Nina Ricci, Madame Grès, and Givenchy. Her atelier, at 327 rue de Saint-Martin, is still in business under the management of Madame Gallet's daughter, who is also the proprietor of a costume jewelry boutique at the Forum des Halles.

The main part of the collar is fashioned from four strands of simulated pearls, reduced to three strands at the upper part of the necklace. Gold-plated spacers, made up of a row of simulated pearls, break up the strands of pearls. Pearl "bridges" define the change from four strands to three and to the clasp, and are part of the massing of colored glass beads for the central cluster.

BROOCH SHAPED LIKE PEA PODS

The freshness of this graceful and unusual brooch is perfectly in line with the Christian Dior style, depicting women as looking natural, elegant, and polished. This brooch, in glass paste outlined with handworked gold-plated metal, is shaped to depict two pea pods sprouting from a small bunch of leaves. One pod contains five glass simulated pearls, and the other has six. The brooch exemplifies a specialty of Maison Gripoix: simulated pearls and glass paste enclosed inside frames outlined with metal to enliven the petals and leaves. Maison Gripoix has been in existence for more than one hundred years and has always been managed by women. Gripoix workmanship has been passed down from mother to daughter and from worker to worker, with the firm's unique methods kept secret. This quality control has allowed this small firm of just over thirty people to become the favorite supplier of some of the greatest couturiers of this century —Charles Frederick Worth, Poiret, Chanel, Dior, Yves Saint-Laurent, and Karl Lagerfeld.

Designer
Suzanne Gripoix

Manufacturer
Gripoix for Christian Dior

Place and Date of Manufacture
France, c. 1955

Materials and Techniques
Glass paste with a gold-plated metal frame, simulated pearls

Mark
None

Provenance
Private collection, Milan

DEMI-PARURE OF NECKLACE AND BUTTON EARRINGS

Designer
Louis Rousselet

Manufacturer
Louis Rousselet for Burma

Place and Date of Manufacture
France, 1955

Materials and Techniques
Glass paste, glass, simulated pearls, burnished-metal components

Mark
None

Provenance
Private collection, New York

As a result of the Great Depression of the 1930s, Rousselet closed its plant in Persan-Beaumont where it had manufactured simulated pearls in glass and metallic components, in large part for the then-diminishing American market. The firm continued to operate at a reduced level until 1972, producing objects made from galalith, straw, raffia, leather, and ceramics. In that year, Louis Rousselet was succeeded by his daughter Denise, who continues to operate out of a small boutique, "Jeanne d'Anjou," on the Pont-Neuf in Paris.

This necklace is composed of alternating pink and green balls held by pins inside a burnished-metal chain track. The pendant is a cluster of small simulated pearls and glass-paste balls and petals in the same pastel shades as the rest of the necklace. Likewise, the pendant tassels are made of similarly colored glass-paste beads. The button earrings pick up on the pendant design of green and pink glass-paste balls and leaves.

CHATELAINE SCARF PIN

Designer
Suzanne Gripoix
Manufacturer
Gripoix for Chanel
Place and Date of Manufacture
France, late 1950s
Materials and Techniques
Glass and glass-paste balls, simulated pearls, small beads, gold-plated metal
Mark
Déposé (on the pin)
Provenance
Private collection

This brooch was identified by Josette Gripoix, the daughter of an assistant to the jewel's creator, Suzanne Gripoix. Suzanne, who succeeded her mother Augustine who was the late nineteenth-century founder of Maison Gripoix, collaborated with Mademoiselle Chanel from the time of Chanel's debut in the field of fashion in the early twenties.

The fastener for the pin is round in shape with a gold-plated metal base covered by a green glass-paste cabochon stone. The cabochon is encircled by a strand of small green, red, and blue glass-paste beads and four gold-plated metal beads. Three small chains composed of simulated baroque pearls and glass-paste balls in red, azure, green, and cobalt blue descend from the colorful fastener. Both the pearls and the glass pastes end in very tiny glass-paste balls in a contrasting color.

CHANEL
LINK BRACELET

Manufacturer
Unknown, for Chanel

**Place and Date
of Manufacture**
France, late 1950s

**Materials and
Techniques**
Punched gold-plated
metal, gold-plated
chain, simulated pearls,
glass-paste balls

Mark
Chanel

Provenance
Private collection

Chanel

Chanel jewelry is identified three ways: signed by Chanel in block capital letters, as it is currently marked; in cursive, with the first letter capitalized; or unsigned. This bracelet is stamped with the mark in cursive, which from a historical point of view is more problematic. In fact, this mark is not registered with any of the appropriate agencies either in France or in the United States. However, in the United States the block capital signature was registered under no. 195360 on February 24, 1925. The current managers of the House of Chanel believe that the cursive mark could have been a take-off of "Gabrielle Chanel," the caption that accompanied her earliest creations, but they have no actual proof.

This bracelet is composed of three rectangular, gold-plated metal plates punched to look like a filigree of dense arabesque ornamentation with a rosette in the center. The plates are separated by round metal rods with simulated pearls and red and green glass-paste beads, each punctuated by a cluster of glass balls. A small chain supports a gold-plated metal scimitar which acts as a catch when slipped into the oblong opening of the fastener.

PIN IN THE SHAPE OF
A VASE OF FLOWERS

C.I.S. is the professional name for Countess Cissy Zoltowska, a Viennese woman with a background in chemistry. Zoltowska began her career as a creator of costume jewelry in Lausanne, where she worked from 1944 to 1951. At that time, she specialized in working in ceramics, creating handmade jewelry and items for the home that were so fine they looked like porcelain. The vase for this brooch was created from a grooved glass-paste stone. The brooch is a succession of gold-plated metal openwork that enclose fuchsia and turquoise glass-paste stones. The flowers are pink glass-paste cabochons.

Designer
Cissy Zoltowska

Manufacturer
Cissy Zoltowska

Place and Date of Manufacture
France, late 1950s

Materials and Techniques
Glass paste, gold-plated metal components

Mark
Déposé (on the pin)
Cis (on the back)

Provenance
Private collection, Los Angeles

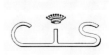

COLLAR OF OVAL MEDALLIONS

Designer
Suzanne Gripoix

Manufacturer
Gripoix

Place and Date of Manufacture
Paris, late 1950s

Materials and Techniques
Simulated pearls made of glass, gold-plated metal, small glass pearls, metal rivets, rhinestones

Mark
None

Provenance
Private collection, New York

This collar necklace is made up of six oval plates, with the sixth being the clasp. The other five support a large drop-shaped simulated pearl. The plates, consisting of a metal gallery held in place by metal prongs, are covered with rounded simulated pearls, attached to the gallery by brass rivets, and pale yellow châton-cut rhinestones in prong settings.

The collar is noteworthy because of the laborious handwork required: each rhinestone of the almost two hundred that make up one of the ovals is held by six hand-bent prongs, and each simulated pearl is fixed in place by inserting a rivet which is, in turn, bent on the back of the gallery so that it stays in the desired position. This clearly demonstrates that it is not only the preciousness of the materials employed that determine the beauty of a piece of jewelry, but how and with what care it is assembled.

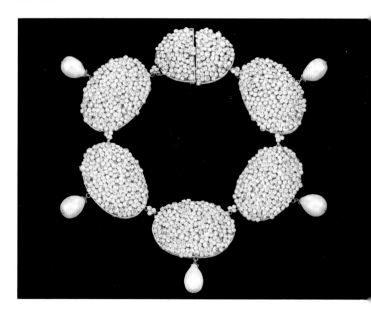

WREATH-STYLE BROOCH

Manufacturer
Madeleine Rivière
for Nina Ricci

**Place and Date
of Manufacture**
Paris, early 1950s

**Materials and
Techniques**
Faceted glass stones,
azure-colored strass,
simulated baroque
pearls

Mark
41 (probably the
model number)

Provenance
Private collection,
Paris

This large pin was identified by Madame Gal-et's daughter, who confirmed that her mother had made it for Maison Ricci. As a matter of fact, the simplicity of the brooch does evoke the style of that great fashion house. Ricci was the creator of unforgettable dresses and per-fumes, exuding a style that favored quality over eccentricity and a refined, bourgeois ele-gance over questionable exhibitionism. The pin depicts a laurel wreath with leaves formed of clear navette-cut stones, châton-cut berries, and azure strass. The shoot was fashioned from brass wires and soldered settings that hold the navette crystals. The branch supports an oval of pearlized, blown glass with a mot-tled, cabochon-style effect. A simulated pearl dangles from the base of the brooch.

CHANEL COLLAR
AND BROOCH

Designer
Suzanne Gripoix

Manufacturer
Gripoix for Chanel

**Place and Date
of Manufacture**
Paris, late 1950s

Materials and Techniques
Glass paste, rhinestones, rhinestone and gold-plated metal rondelles

Mark
None

Provenance
Private collection

The brooch depicts a camellia, one of Chanel's favorite flowers, which became the emblem of her style and was fashioned in materials such as silk, plastic, voile, and chintz. Here the flower is white glass paste with a rhinestone in the center and five lanceolate leaves made of green glass paste.

The main part of the necklace is composed of a series of corollas, with two petals made of gold-plated bent wire enclosing a large rhinestone in a prong setting, and four glass-paste petals in alternating shades of blue and green. The back part of the necklace has alternating blue and green glass-paste beads interposed with metal and rhinestone rondelles. Both the brooch and the necklace are emblematic of the dramatic beauty that Chanel looked for in her jewels. As she said, "Costume jewelry is not made to give women an aura of wealth, but to make them beautiful." This necklace is pictured on page 125 of J. Mulvagh's *Costume Jewelry in Vogue*, published by Thames & Hudson, New York, in 1988.

PARURE WITH INTERTWINED BANDS

Lina Baretti, who was born in Ajaccio in 1900 and died in Paris in 1990, was a pianist in her youth and socialized with all of Paris. Later on, through the end of the seventies, she devoted herself to making costume jewelry for the couture industry in her atelier at number 9 rue Anatole de la Forge in Paris. Baretti made her debut with Madeleine Vionnet and subsequently added Schiaparelli, Chanel, Molyneux, Dior, and Balenciaga to her list of clientele. She created exclusive jewelry for the Duchess of Windsor and a few other important private clients. Endowed with an unparalleled sense of invention, she used feathers, trimmings, glass paste, silk, and velvet in unforgettable combinations.

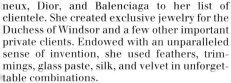

The style of this parure consists of intertwined bands of gold-plated metal to which black velvet ribbons have been pasted. The edges of the ribbons are defined by thin strands of tinsel and a row of *roses montées*. The bands end in a hub made of a glass-paste ball simulating coral. This is a typical example of a *bijou de couture*, executed entirely by hand and in a limited number of copies, with a choice of colors and materials designed to enhance both the dress and the rosy tones of the wearer's skin.

Designer
Lina Baretti

Manufacturer
Lina Baretti

Place and Date of Manufacture
France, late 1950s

Materials and Techniques
Metal and velvet, worked *roses montées*, tinsel

Mark
None

Provenance
Private collection

SQUARED PLAQUE NECKLACE

Designer
Lola Prusac

Manufacturer
Unknown, for Lola
Prusac

**Place and Date
of Manufacture**
Paris, late 1950s

**Materials and
Techniques**
Silver-plated stamped
metal, silver-plated
chain, glass paste

Mark
None

Provenance
Private collection,
Paris

Lola Prusac was a woman of Polish descent who
in 1910 arrived in Paris where she attended the
Ecole des Beaux-Arts. She began her career
with Hermès in 1927 as a style consultant. In
1935 she opened her own boutique where she
specialized in haute couture outfits and accessories created in materials that were considered
strange at the time, such as leather and string.

Prusac worked closely with established
artisans like Simone Dumas, who excelled at
costume jewelry. The necklaces and bracelets
conceived by Prusac are in hammered or polished silver, bronze, or gold-plated metal and
were inspired by the ethnic jewelry she saw on
her trips to Egypt, Greece, and India. Only the
silver jewelry is signed M. C. Lola Prusac. She
stopped working in 1982 and was succeeded
by her grandson, who carries on at her boutique at 36 rue La Vrillière.

This necklace is stamped silver-plated
metal with a double-linked chain joined to
square articulated plaques.

GOLD-PLATED BROOCHES

Jeanne Péral opened her costume jewelry atelier in 1939 in Paris at 21 rue d'Hauteville. Devoted to traditional artisan's methods, Péral surrounded herself with a group of about a dozen workers and prepared her first jewels, which evoked classical Greek and Etruscan jewelry, for Schiaparelli. A great traveler, Péral drew inspiration from every country she visited and brought back precious materials—Chinese coral, turquoise, Tibetan stones, agate, horn, and ivory—that she then used in her work. Péral launched the vogue for semiprecious stones in haute couture, working for Balenciaga, Givenchy, Courrèges, Scherrer, Balmain, Yves Saint-Laurent, Ungaro, and Dior. In fact, she worked for Dior for over twenty-five years. In 1989 she closed her atelier which had by then relocated to 17 rue Saints-Pères.

The five-petaled flower brooch is metal that has been partially cold-enameled. The remainder of the flower was engraved with a burin in order to create a slight granulation. The square brooch presents a surface of sixteen circular patterns in relief on a blue background, arranged in four rows and decorated with abstract symbols and signs of the zodiac.

Designer
Jeanne Péral

Manufacturer
Jeanne Péral

Place and Date of Manufacture
France, late 1950s

Materials and Techniques
Partly enameled, gold-plated stamped metal

Mark
None

Provenance
Private collection

DIOR COLLAR

Designer
Christian Dior
Manufacturer
Henkel & Grosse for
Christian Dior
**Place and Date
of Manufacture**
Pforzheim (Germany),
1958
**Materials and
Techniques**
Stamped glass
paste, rhinestones,
silver-plated metal
components
Mark
C. Dior 1958
Provenance
Private collection

In contrast to Dior's style of clothing, his *bijoux de couture* are only rarely traditional and this only as regards the jewels he uses—they are never traditional in either materials or colors. In fact, it appears that the very basis of their conception for Dior is the desire to "break away" from the conservative elegance of his outfits. The "natural" colors of precious stones are not the colors that Dior preferred for his costume jewelry. On the contrary, he chose violet-browns with golden highlights, irides-cent colors, and shocking pink.

This necklace is composed of nine semicir-cular segments made with two different colors of glass paste (light and dark orange), stamped in the shape of leaves. The glass-paste stones are mounted in prong settings and are inter-posed with châton-cut blue rhinestones. The clasp is a silver-plated metal chain. The neck-lace's incredible plastic effect is the result of skillfully concealing the settings, stone by stone, through careful hand labor.

DIOR SAPPHIRE CHOKER
WITH RHINESTONE CHAIN

Revivals recur so often in the history of costume ornaments that it is difficult to precisely date some pieces. But upon careful examination, small details often help settle the date. The rhinestone chain, for example, was patented in the second half of the fifties. Therefore, given the presence of this material, this necklace could only have been made after the date of the patent.

Designer
Christian Dior
Manufacturer
Henkel & Grosse for Christian Dior
Place and Date of Manufacture
Pforzheim, 1958
Materials and Techniques
Glass stones
Mark
C. Dior 1958
Provenance
Private collection

DIOR PARURE
WITH SIMULATED RUBIES

Designer
Christian Dior

Manufacturer
Henkel & Grosse for
Christian Dior

**Place and Date
of Manufacture**
Pforzheim (Germany),
1959

**Materials and
Techniques**
Silver-plated metal components, faceted glass
stones simulating rubies,
glass simulated pearls

Mark
C. Dior 1959

Provenance
Private collection, Milan

The coupling of the names Christian Dior and Henkel & Grosse (now Grosse Jewels) lasted from 1955 until the great master couturier's death. Today, Grosse Jewels continues to produce jewelry for Maison Dior.

This collar necklace is composed of a strand of red châton-cut glass stones, simulating rubies, with prong settings and metal links. Round glass stones alternate with glass stones of the same color which are either navette-cut or drop-cut. The stones are mounted to form two leafy garlands connected by a row of graduated, glass simulated pearls. Numerous prong-set, red glass stones are arranged in a wreath-like frame around the large glass simulated pearl in the center of the brooch.

BALENCIAGA COLLAR IN PASTEL COLORS

Robert Goossens, whose father was a caster of bronze art objects, was born in 1927 and was familiar with artisan techniques at an early age. He began his apprenticeship in 1942 with a jeweler named Bauer, who at the time worked exclusively for Cartier. Gradually, through his experience working with the greatest jewelers in Paris—Lefebvre, Berchot, the Dupuis brothers (the engravers for the Palais Royal), and finally Max Boinet, who at the time was creating costume jewelry for Schiaparelli—he perfected his skills as an artisan-artist.

From his experiences with Boinet, Goossens began to establish a relationship with the fashion jewelry world and eventually became Coco Chanel's favorite creator from 1958 until her death. Today, Goossens's creations are available at the R. Goossen boutique at 42 avenue George V.

This collar necklace is composed entirely of pastel-colored faceted crystals of different cuts and sizes, mounted in prong settings fashioned from silver-plated metal. The main part is made up of a triangular central motif—with violet, pink, and white faceted crystals cut into oval, rectangular, and round shapes. The corners of the base of the triangle are two smaller pendants also in the pastel-colored crystals. A pattern of châton-cut clear crystal, set in an individual prong-setting, and two smaller pink crystals form the balance of the necklace.

Designer
Robert Goossens

Manufacturer
Robert Goossens for Balenciaga

Place and Date of Manufacture
France, late 1950s

Materials and Techniques
Faceted crystals, handworked metal components

Mark
Made in France

Provenance
Private collection, Florence

V-SHAPED CRYSTAL BRACELET

Designer
Lyda Coppola

Manufacturer
Coppola & Toppo for
Elsa Schiaparelli

**Place and Date
of Manufacture**
Italy, 1952

**Materials and
Techniques**
Crystals sewn on a
gold-plated metal
gallery, brass base

Mark
Made in Italy by
Coppola & Toppo

Provenance
Private collection

This bracelet—shown by Bettina, a famous
model in the fifties—was published in the November 15, 1952 American issue of *Vogue* as
one of Elsa Schiaparelli's jewels. As a matter of
fact, it is one of Lyda Coppola's creations for
Coppola & Toppo. But as with all *bijoux de couture*, the name that is attached to a piece of jewelry is that of the couturier who selected it for
a collection. In the same way, the names of so
many talented artisans who devoted themselves to making eyeglasses, ornaments, accessories, fabrics, and decorative objects for the
home were replaced by the names of the people who selected their products. In the majority of cases, the name of the person who designs
and makes products for a third party is known
only to a few insiders who will do everything
they can to suppress the maker's name.

This V-shaped bracelet is composed of different sizes of multicolored crystals sewn to
an underlying metal gallery. Rows of Venetian
glass seed beads in the same colors fill in the
spaces between the crystals.

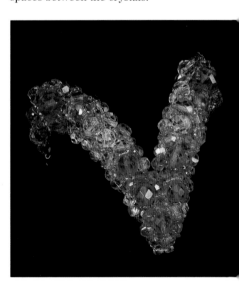

MULTISTRAND WHITE-AND-YELLOW NECKLACE

Designer
Emma Caimi Pellini

Manufacturer
Emma Caimi Pellini

Place and Date of Manufacture
Italy, 1952

Materials and Techniques
Glass-paste beads and stones, gold-plated metal inserts, stones sewn on a metal gallery

Mark
None

Provenance
Donatella Pellini Archive, Milan

Emma Caimi Pellini was one of the first firms to distinguish itself in the years following the war when it introduced its Venetian glass jewelry. In 1951, the firm was invited to participate in the exhibition of Italian fashion organized by Giorgini at the Palazzo Pitti in Florence. From that moment on, the firm expanded at a remarkable rate, thanks to a large number of orders from the United States where, in 1952, Emma Caimi Pellini participated in the New York Fair of Italian Manufactures. At present, the firm is managed by the founder's grandchildren, Donatella and Ernesto, who have raised their products to an international level, especially in Japan.

The back part of the necklace is three strands of smooth, white glass-paste beads. In the main part of the piece, the strand in the middle is composed of white glass paste shaped like smooth hemispheres—with gold-plated metal inserts—and grooved ovals and balls. The strands on the outside contain irregular ovals of glass paste, interspaced with groups of three flattened, white glass-paste stones. The clasp, shaped like a flower with six petals, is formed of white glass-paste beads sewn on a metal gallery.

DUAL-PURPOSE NECKLACE

Designer
Giuliano Fratti

Manufacturer
Unknown, for Giuliano Fratti

Place and Date of Manufacture
Italy, early 1950s

Materials and Techniques
Glass simulated pearls, silver-plated metal, rhinestones, synthetic stones

Mark
None

Provenance
Civiche Raccolte d'Arti Applicate, Milan

In the fifties, with sporty dresses and ankle-length skirts almost totally nonexistent, women adopted a dressy, refined style. Having tempered the asymmetry, irregularity, and unexpected lines desired by French couturiers, Italian designers employed asymmetrical details, especially in their skirts. Costume jewelry was also rich in references to Edwardian style, but nonetheless graceful.

This necklace of two strands of glass simulated pearls is good evidence of this new Italian style. The two large clasps are significant because they can also be detached and used as brooches. Each is made of two silver-plated metal units covered with châton-cut clear rhinestones, arranged around a large cylindrical stone, made of a green-colored synthetic material, placed in the center of each unit.

COLLAR WITH PEARL TASSELS

The attribution of this piece to Luciana Aloisi de Reutern is based on a few bits of concrete data. The necklace was purchased in America and few Italian ornaments of the fifties made by firms other than Luciana, Fratti, or Coppola & Toppo reached these shores. Furthermore, based on the classical style of the necklace, Luciana comes to mind. According to Irene Brin, Luciana "studies enormous amounts of ancient art in order to draw from them the delicate booty for a single earring."

This necklace is a gold-plated metal chain of flat links and six tassels; each tassel is composed of eight strands of glass simulated pearls. The pearls increase in size from the base outwards. The pearl strands are joined inside a hollow, gold-plated metal cap adorned with an oval stone made of turquoise-colored glass paste. The tassels are suspended from the chain by oval links. The necklace was shown at the exhibit "Ad Onor del Falso," held in Rome at the Palazzo delle Esposizioni from June 4 to July 26, 1993.

Designer
Probably Luciana
Aloisi de Reutern

Manufacturer
Probably Luciana
Aloisi de Reutern

Place and Date of Manufacture
Italy, early 1950s

Materials and Techniques
Gold-plated chain, simulated pearls, glass-paste stones, gold-plated metal components

Mark
Italy (on the chain)

Provenance
Private collection

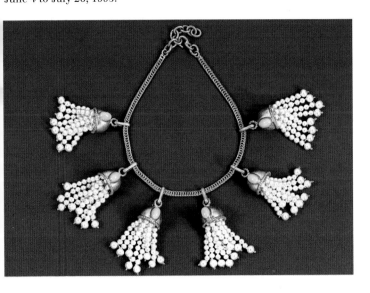

CERAMIC BROOCH
WITH A SERPENT

Designer
Maria Vittoria Albani

Manufacturer
Ornella

**Place and Date
of Manufacture**
Milan, early 1950s

**Materials and
Techniques**
Triple-fired earthenware, painted, enameled, and gold-plated; gold-plated metal components; cultivated pearl and faceted glass stone

Mark
None

Provenance
Ornella Archives, Milan

The serpent, symbol of all that is rare, mysterious, and incomprehensible to the human mind, and at the same time, symbol of the supernatural and of eternity, is a long-treasured subject in jewelry design. This brooch depicts a serpent curled up in an "S" shape, supporting a large pendant made up of a gold-plated metal base. The principal material used for this brooch is triple-fired earthenware that has been painted, enameled, and gold-plated. The inserts—a large blue faceted stone held by a gold-plated metal setting with a trefoil border and two coral-colored stones—are made from glass. A cultured pearl is lodged in the center of the pendant. Both the material and the techniques employed to create the serpent were a specialty of the Ornella Company throughout the fifties.

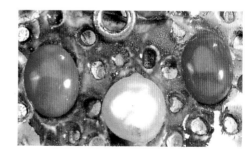

STYLIZED CERAMIC DEMI-PARURE

Faenza is a name that has been known throughout the Western world since the sixteenth century, when Faenza-style majolica production, whose origins date to the twelfth

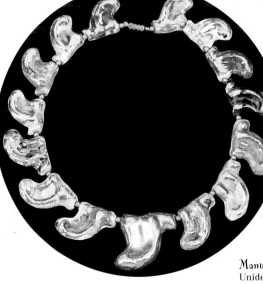

century, spread throughout Europe and took on the French name *faience*. Ceramic jewelry like the necklace and brooch seen here were also Faenza-style production. Ceramic decorative objects were very popular in the fifties, not only in Italy but in all of Europe and the United States, largely as a consequence of the scarcity of Austrian and Czech stones in the postwar years. Moreover, the ease, immediacy, and pliability of working with ceramics reintroduced a style that met with aesthetic approbation.

Manufacturer
Unidentified, for Furla (Bologna)

Place and Date of Manufacture
Faenza (Italy), early 1950s

Materials and Techniques
Gold-plated painted ceramics, metal screw clasp

Mark
None

Provenance
Veronica Guiduzzi Collection, Bologna

RIGID NECKLACE WITH THREE LEAVES

Designer
Emy Manca

Manufacturer
Bijoux Bozart

Place and Date of Manufacture
Italy, late 1950s

Materials and Techniques
Stamped metal, silver-plated, copper-plated, and burnished; wire

Mark
None

Provenance
Bijoux Bozart Archive, Milan

This type of rigid necklace, with a stem and leaves, greatly recalls the jewelry of Paul Flauto, an American designer of the forties. The stars loved the sober elegance and simplicity of his jewels, which were often imitated by costume jewelry manufacturers like Marcel Boucher. Bijoux Bozart was started in 1956 in Milan at the initiative of Emy and Giuseppe Manca. By the sixties, the firm had already established a relationship with the most important Italian fashion houses, producing for them costume jewelry that was characterized by good formal research, even into trends from abroad, and the finest of craftsmanship. At present, Bozart is managed by the son of the founders, Maurizio Manca. The firm's products are primarily sold out of its store in Milan at 8 Corso Vittorio Emanuele.

This necklace originates from a very simple structure: a semirigid wire (known as a spring wire) representing the stem, with a small metal ball at one end which constitutes the curved back part of the necklace. Three lanceolate leaves, made of rosy-colored metal that has been silver-plated and burnished, make up the main part of the necklace.

LAMP-BEAD COLLAR

Given that since antiquity Venice has been one of the three most important centers for glass production in the world, it seems incredible that there is no specific single Italian word to define a "glass ball for stringing" other than "pearl," which in that language refers to the pearl produced by oysters.

Despite having been made from a traditional material like Venetian beads, a material used in great abundance for souvenir jewelry, the necklace below is quite graceful and has a remarkable visual impact. It is far removed from the banality of souvenirs, which rarely change, and is in harmony with the classical revival style of the fifties. This festooned necklace is composed of twenty-five drop-shaped polychrome lamp beads, in alternating yellow and green colors, strung with matching lamp beads.

Place and Date of Manufacture
Venice, late 1950s

Materials and Techniques
Polychrome lamp beads

Mark
None

Provenance
Private collection, Venice

DEMI-PARURE WITH STYLIZED FLORAL MOTIFS

Manufacturer
Unidentified, for the
Gablonzer Genossen-
schaft Cooperative

Place and Date of Manufacture
Neugablonz (Austria),
late 1950s

Materials and Techniques
Glass stones, burnished
metal components

Mark
None

Provenance
Donatella Pellini
Collection, Milan

The Gablonzer Genossenschaft is the cooperative for Austrian producers of fashion jewelry
and a few manufacturers of imitation stones. It
was founded in 1947 in Neugablonz, where a
new community was established made up of
specialists in working with glass and its derivatives, primarily emigrants from what is now
Jablonec Nad Nisou in the Czech Republic.
These manufacturers often create jewelry for
important French and German fashion houses,
but at the express wish of their clients the
manufacturers do not divulge the names of
these houses.

The necklace below is composed of stylized flowers fashioned from an assemblage of
navette-, pear-, châton-, or carré-cut opaque
glass stones in shades of violet, pink, and green.
Metal links connect the stones. The clasp is
composed of a snap link along an adjustable
chain. The earrings match the necklace.

GILDED AND ENAMELED
LINK BRACELET

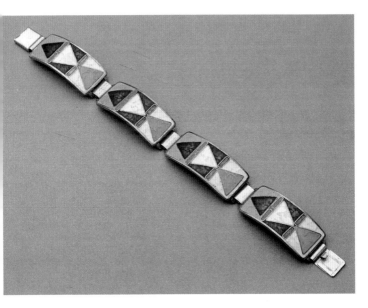

Perli Pearl Industries of Schwäbisch Gmünd was founded in the early twenties by Martha May and specialized in the manufacturing of glass-pearl costume jewelry. In 1937 the firm won a silver medal at the Paris Exposition. Two years later, it reached its maximum size, employing over 100 workers. In addition to wood, glass, and porcelain beads, Perli's production also included objects made from pewter or silver. From 1935 on, they also made enameled ornaments which were later to become their specialty. Today the firm is still in operation under the direction of Peter and Guido May.

This bracelet is composed of four slightly arched plaques of gold-plated tombac divided into triangular decorative patterns created by polychrome opaque cold-enameling in green, blue, brown, and ivory, with gold-colored edging and bands. The connecting pieces and clasp are also made up of gold-plated tombac.

Manufacturer
Perli

Place and Date of Manufacture
Schwäbisch Gmünd (Germany), c. 1955

Materials and Techniques
Silver-plated and enameled tombac

Mark
PE

Provenance
Private collection, Vienna

CRACKLEWARE COLLAR

Place and Date of Manufacture
Denmark, late 1950s

Materials and Techniques
Crackleware, stamped silver

Mark
Sterling Denmark

Provenance
Private collection

This necklace is an example of the interesting alternatives found in the Nordic countries, resulting from the rationing of precious and semiprecious metals and the lack of imitation stones from Austria and Czechoslovakia during the Second World War. These solutions, perfected over the years, gave rise to a kind of costume jewelry typical of these countries, characterized by abstract designs and a remarkable use of enamels. This collar is composed of twenty-five trapezoidal pieces of ceramic painted in different shades of violet that when fired produce a crackled effect on the surface. The ceramic pieces are connected by small silver rods strung on nylon thread.

NONFIGURATIVE BURNISHED SILVER BROOCH

Manufacturer
J. Tostrup, Norway

Place and Date of Manufacture
Norway, late 1950s

Materials and Techniques
Burnished, stamped, and cut silver

Mark
Sterling Norway, manufacturer's intials

Provenance
Private collection

This stamped-silver brooch, cut and burnished, has an abstract shape with cutaway holes that shows the influence of the avant-garde on the manufacturers of fashion ornaments. By the 1930s, these manufacturers had become common in the Nordic countries.

In the fifties, nonrepresentational art, in a variety of artistic interpretations, made a name for itself at the international level. Its principles, passed from one country to the next, were reflected in all areas—furniture, fabrics, dresses, even fashion jewelry. As a painting is a structure of lines, and color is itself a form in nonrepresentational art, so an ornament also becomes a pure representation of itself. Here, the theme of this brooch is simply the play of empty and full spaces.

PAIR OF BLUE ENAMELED BROOCHES

Manufacturer
David Andersen

Place and Date of Manufacture
Norway, early 1950s

Materials and Techniques
Cast fire-enameled silver

Mark
D.A.; 925 S

Provenance
Ilene Chazanof Collection, New York

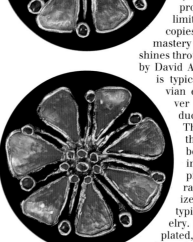

The long history of the Andersen dynasty of silversmiths and jewelry creators began in 1876 with its founder David, who was succeeded by his sons Alfred and Arthur David. David Andersen's grandson Ivar and great-grandson John Arthur continued in the business, as well as Uni and Ben David, two of the few women who managed silver workshops specializing in one-of-a-kind objects and jewelry produced in a limited number of copies. The firm's mastery of its craft shines through in this work by David Andersen, which is typical of Scandinavian enamel and silver jewelry produced in the fifties. The rendering of the subject also bears a personal imprint, as the piece is rough rather than stylized and flat like typical fifties jewelry. It is also gold-plated, not silver-plated, and naturalistic in style instead of abstract. In a word, the work is inspired by tradition rather than by avant-garde art movements.

The brooches were made from a cast of cobalt blue fire-enameled silver, shaped to depict a corolla of flowers with seven petals. The enamel on the petals is blue brightened with silvery touches, while the pistils in the center and along the sides are enameled in midnight blue.

BICOLOR ENAMELED BROOCH

The predominant characteristic of work executed in the Scandinavian countries is a mastery of form rather than a pronounced color sense. This purity of line, well represented by the brooch illustrated above, became a conscious choice, expressed with force at a time when anything, even the most intricate object, could be created using machines.

The creator of this brooch, Juliane Pfeiffer, who works for the jeweler Bolin in Stockholm, is an artisan with considerable experience in jewelry making. The base of the brooch is metal that has been enameled in two colors. Its spheroid, bombé shape is highlighted by irregular bands of blue enamel on a red-orange background. Its plasticity expresses a surrealistic tendency.

Designer
Juliane Pfeiffer

Manufacturer
Juliane Pfeiffer

Place and Date of Manufacture
Sweden, c. 1950

Materials and Techniques
Enameled metal

Mark
J. P.

Provenance
Private collection, Vienna

BROOCH WITH POLYCHROME ENAMEL INSERTS

Manufacturer
Balle

Place and Date of Manufacture
Norway, c. 1955

Materials and Techniques
Gold plate and partially fire-enameled silver

Mark
Balle, 925 Sterling, Norway

Provenance
Ilene Chazanof Collection, New York

The isolation of the Scandinavian peninsula during the war years and the resulting scarcity of materials for jewelry and ornaments (gold, silver, precious and imitation stones were all imported materials) made it necessary to use indigenous products (bone, iron, bronze, and oak) coupled with alternative ways of creating spots of color. The first nonprecious enameled ornament, an ornament that gained notoriety because it had one of the highest sales records for an individual object, was designed and executed in 1940 by A. Michelsen; it was called "Margherita" in honor of the princess born that same year. The decade that followed produced many other beautiful specimens of enameled ornaments.

This brooch is gold-plated metal in a molded, quadrilobate shape. Decorative inserts of sky blue, red, and black polychrome fired enamel animate the brooch.

COPPER AND ENAMEL BRACELETS

These bracelets are hinged, with the exception of the one at the upper right, and are executed in copper with copper inlay. They were first silver-plated to assure good results from the enamel, which was painted in layers and baked at a high temperature. Typical fifties patterns similar to those made with enamel can also be found in clothing fabrics and home furnishings.

Although abstraction became a dominant movement in art after World War II, representation was still popular with the general public. For these bracelets, which were intended to appeal to a broad range of women and to be sold at moderate cost at the express wish of Renoir's owner, softer and more familiar designs were sought. The palette is brighter than it generally is in painting and is always in harmony with the main material, the copper, with its warm, decorative rosy, color that has been treated so it will remain unchanged over time. At a distance of forty years, this is a fully realized goal.

Designer
Jerry Felds

Manufacturer
Renoir of California

Place and Date of Manufacture
Los Angeles, early 1950s

Materials and Techniques
Copper, partially fire-enameled

Mark
"Matisse Renoir"

Provenance
Private collection

PAIR OF CHATELEINE BROOCHES

Manufacturer
Leo Glass &
Company, Inc.

**Place and Date
of Manufacture**
New York, early 1950s

**Materials and
Techniques**
Stamped-metal chain
and components, gold-
plated and partially
cold-enameled;
engraved, round
glass-paste stone

Mark
Leo Glass

Provenance
Private collection

Leo Glass & Company, Inc. was established in
1943 at 389 Fifth Avenue in New York as a factory for fashion jewelry. Their products were a
great commercial success, and in 1949 they
opened a second office at 16 West 36th Street.
The first sign of the firm's decline occurred in
1952 when it cut back to one office; in 1957 the
firm went out of business.

These two brooches are patterned after
Victorian sentimental jewelry (the hand grip-
ping the heart, the star-shaped ornamentation,
and the engraved stone) and are an expression
of the revivalism that marked the fifties.
Classic motifs were re-presented and made
with contemporary materials (the links for the
chain, for example, are also taken from old
patterns but are fashioned in larger sizes) to
create new charms to be mixed with those one
already owned.

Leo Glass

SMALL ANIMAL-SHAPED PINS

TRIFARI

Very often a person who approaches the world of costume jewelry for the first time would like to have some advice on how to put together a collection. One suggestion might be to collect objects either by subject (flowers, animals, figures, hearts, etc.), or by style (Art Nouveau, Art Déco, the thirties, and so forth), or even by material (Bakelite, silver, enamel, or lucite).

This group of pins is an example of the beginning of a collection centered around the theme of animals from the same period and created by the same manufacturer, Trifari, who even with objects of a small size maintains its usual level of quality and careful workmanship. This group of nine small pins depicts an elephant, a chick, an owl, a frog, a miniature poodle, a bird, and a duckling. Each of the animals' bellies is a glass stone that is either flat and faceted or rounded and smooth like a cabochon.

Pavé-set rhinestones and eyes, fashioned from round glass-paste stones, are used for some of the animals. Baguette-cut stones are often used on the limbs and tails.

Designer
Alfred Philippe

Manufacturer
Trifari, Krussman & Fishel

Place and Date of Manufacture
United States, c. 1951

Materials and Techniques
Cast gold-plated metal, glass stones, rhinestones

Mark
Trifari

Provenance
Epoque Collection, Bologna

LARGE BROOCH SHAPED LIKE MUSICAL NOTES

Designer
Francisco Rebajes

Manufacturer
Francisco Rebajes

**Place and Date
of Manufacture**
New York, early 1950s

**Materials and
Techniques**
Stamped copper

Mark
Rebajes

Provenance
Private collection

This brooch bears witness to Rebajes's tendency toward a sculptural rendering of a subject in humble but brilliant materials like copper, which in his hands takes on a sense of life and movement achieved by no other manufacturer. Francisco Rebajes was born to Spanish parents in 1906 in Puerto Palta in the Dominican Republic. After studying for a few years in Barcelona, he moved to New York in 1923 to try his luck. For a few years he led the life of a gypsy and only occasionally found work. Then he met the woman who was to become his wife and she helped to bring out the best in him. So he became an artist. In 1937 he won a medal of honor at the Paris Exposition Universelle, and in 1939 he designed six murals for the United States pavillion at the New York World's Fair. His star continued to rise, and in 1943 he opened a shop on Fifth Avenue that was to become one of the favorite meeting places for New York intellectuals.

NECKLACE, BRACELET, AND EARRINGS PARURE

Turquoise and white were the preferred colors for jewelry in the fifties; ornaments which were to become bigger and bigger as if to draw attention away from the dresses with their strange, unprecedented shapes (trapeze, sack, and balloon).

The bracelet and necklace in this parure are formed of silver-plated chains with a few pendants fashioned from wire. The wire was bent to form a cone ending in a spiral from which a grooved, turquoise-colored glass-paste stone is suspended. The necklace chain is divided in two segments of unequal length. The short side, used to make a half turn around the neck, connects to the longer segment on the other side of the clasp. The longer side hangs down and forms the center of the necklace where the graduated pendants are hung.

The hanging earrings are cone-shaped pendants in silver-plated metal with a suspended glass-paste grooved ball.

Manufacturer
Napier

Place and Date of Manufacture
United States,
early 1950s

Materials and Techniques
Chain and components in stamped bent wire, grooved glass-paste balls

Mark
Napier

Provenance
Private collection, Milan

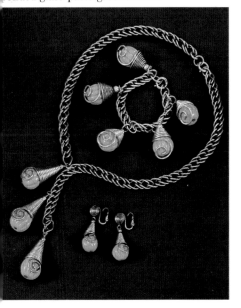

NAPIER

CHATELAINE
BROOCH

Manufacturer
Unknown, for Adele
Simpson

**Place and Date
of Manufacture**
New York, late 1950s

**Materials and
Techniques**
Stamped gold-plated
metal, glass paste,
gold-plated metal

Mark
Adele Simpson

Provenance
Virginia Fuentes
Collection, New York

This brooch is an effective example of Victorian revival and emphasizes Adele Simpson's predilection for classic motifs that make her jewelry timeless and suitable for all occasions. Two oval settings holding turquoise-colored glass-paste cabochons are soldered side-by-side to a square, gold-plated metal frame stamped with filigree. The cabochons each have a silver-colored bow achieved by triple firing. A series of large, supple, bossed rectangular links in gold-plated metal hang from the base of the filigreed square. A vertical succession of three more oval settings with cabochons, the same as those in the upper part of the brooch, are soldered to the rectangular links. A drop-shaped pendant in stamped gold-plated metal is attached to the bottom link. From the sides of the square frame that serves as the fastener for the brooch hang gold-plated chains which enliven the line of the piece.

Adele Simpson

NECKLACE WITH A MYTHOLOGICAL PENDANT

Peruzzi Jewel Shop was a firm founded in Boston by Gino Peruzzi in the early thirties. In 1945, though it kept its trade name, the business was sold to Aldo Fioravanti who managed it until it went out of business in 1981.

The chain for this necklace has a variety of stamped decorative designs: masks, a six-petal corolla, and a stylized bellflower. Links connect each of them.

The pendant, which also acts as a brooch, was inspired by an important piece of jewelry held by the British Museum that depicts a mythological subject, *The Judgement of Paris*. Priam's son, surrounded by Hera, Athena, and Aphrodite, holds an apple as he hesitates in deciding which goddess is the most beautiful and should be given that mythical fruit.

Myths are rarely depicted on jewelry, perhaps because of the difficulties involved in making a story comprehensible with a single image. However, figurative subjects like flowers, animals, or hearts abound, as they are simpler to make and more evocative of their sentimental connotations.

Manufacturer
Peruzzi Jewel Shop

Place and Date of Manufacture
Boston, 1950–1960

Materials and Techniques
Cast pendant and stamped silver chain

Mark
Sterling Peruzzi Boston

Provenance
Private collection

PERUZZI BOSTON

DEMI-PARURE WITH TORCHON-STYLE STONES

Manufacturer
Miriam Haskell Jewels

Place and Date of Manufacture
New York, c. 1955

Materials and Techniques
Torchon-style stones, probably French; wire; rhinestone rondelles; spacers and small chains in gold-plated metal

Mark
Miriam Haskell

Provenance
Lo Scrigno del Tempo Collection, Avellino, Italy

Miriam Haskell's deliberate decision to avoid imitating the conventions of jewelry making when creating her *bijoux de couture* is obvious in this parure. The stones have acid colors constructed by an eccentric hand, that aren't found in natural stones. The gold-plating on the metal components is deliberately antiqued so as to seem more bewitching to a person familiar with objects patinated over time. In an interview in 1934, Haskell said: "My jewels are for a new era. They don't belong to the past rather their design reflects the spirit of modern times, in harmony with the beauty and distinction of today's fashions."

This necklace is composed of spring wire that alternates pairs of veined, yellow glass pastes, stamped torchon-style, with rhinestone rondelles and green glass-paste balls. The connecting units are in the form of palmettes with antiqued, gold-plated metal finishings. Two small chains with green glass-paste balls, veined yellow ones, and a small metal ball covered with rhinestones dangle from the necklace. Hanging earrings are similarly designed.

EGYPTIAN-STYLE DEMI-PARURE

The work of Miriam Haskell and her right-hand man Frank Hess, who in his capacity as chief designer bore his share of responsibility for the firm's success from the early thirties until 1952, reveals a profound knowledge of the history of the jewel in its varied manifestations in different periods and cultures. This demi-parure, for example, makes an obvious reference to the Egyptian decorative objects included in the exhibition "Egyptian Treasures 1840 B.C.–1940 A.D." held in 1940 at the Metropolitan Museum of Art in New York.

The necklace is composed of wide bands of glass pastes in alternating colors and arranged like a collar. Rounds of red glass accent the form: two in azure and blue tones, and one in the middle with flat ovals of stamped orange glass. The connecting units are capped and the rectangular clasp with gold-plated metal balls is encircled by a strand of small gold-plated metal beads. The hanging cluster earrings repeat the same chromatic tones as in the necklace; the circular setting with a blue glass paste on the fastener supports red inserts, rounds of gold-plated metal, ovals in alternating red and azure, and blue cabochons.

Manufacturer
Miriam Haskell Jewels

Place and Date of Manufacture
New York, c. 1955

Materials and Techniques
Glass-paste balls, gold-plated metal components

Mark
Miriam Haskell

Provenance
Lo Scrigno del Tempo Collection, Avellino, Italy

FLORAL
DEMI-PARURE

Manufacturer
Miriam Haskell Jewels

**Place and Date
of Manufacture**
New York, c. 1955

**Materials and
Techniques**
Glass paste, gold-plated
metal components

Mark
Miriam Haskell

Provenance
Virginia Fuentes
Collection, New York

For years Miriam Haskell received accolades
in the press for the beauty of her jewelry
and quality of its workmanship. One reviewer
enthused about the "originality of the design,
the impeccable fittings, the quality of her
pearls, a hand-craftsmanship that comes from
long practice, the inviting colors, the interesting and always different shapes of the stones,
also made by hand, their timeless charm...."
The last comment addresses the most striking
characteristic of Haskell's jewelry: its time-
lessness, which is well represented in this set.

The brooch depicts a flower and buds in
orange-red glass paste with an undulating
surface and a leafy shoot. The corolla of the
flower and the leaves are gold-plated metal
stamped with veining. An orange-red glass
paste makes up the center of the button earrings and is edged with gently curved bands of
gold-plated metal.

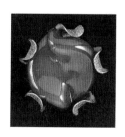

COLLAR MADE OF THREE STRANDS OF BAROQUE PEARLS

Pearls, which according to legend are the tears of stars, seduced by the siren's false promises, that have fallen into the sea, have enjoyed unfailing popularity since antiquity; a success that is justified by the fact that they radiate light. Pearls have a seductive charm and can be worn any time of the day by women young and old, blond or brunette, and need no extra ornamentation. In short, they are absolutely the most sought-after jewels for elegant women. The pearls used for costume jewelry created by Miriam Haskell came from the Orient and were made exclusively for her. Miriam Haskell's pearl jewelry, which even today can be identified by its satiny hues, is for the woman who wishes to look distinguished and whose purchase is like an investment that only improves over time.

This necklace is three strands of glass baroque pearls, larger in size on the outermost strand and accented by gold-plated metal spacers. The clasp is a large, flattened, simulated pearl placed in the center of leafy shoots of gold-plated metal and a stylized, floral ornamental design of small simulated pearls.

Manufacturer
Miriam Haskell Jewels

Place and Date of Manufacture
New York, c. 1955

Materials and Techniques
Glass simulated baroque pearls, gold-plated metal components

Mark
Miriam Haskell

Provenance
Private collection

BROOCH IN THE SHAPE OF A FLOWER

Designer
Marcel Boucher

Manufacturer
Marcel Boucher & Cie

Place and Date of Manufacture
United States, late 1950s

Materials and Techniques
Cast gold-plated metal, rhinestones, baguettes

Mark
C Boucher 7713P

Provenance
Private collection

Among the many manufacturers of ornaments for fashion, Marcel Boucher is certainly the closest in style, subject, and interpretive ability to designers of real jewelry, among whom he learned his craft when he worked as an apprentice to Cartier in the early twenties before he emigrated to the United States.

This brooch, part of a demi-parure, recalls the best in 1950s jewelry production; a sober and elegant naturalism prevails in the jewelry's wavy, three-dimensional lines. The brooch depicts a flower with six highly animated, irregular petals made of châton-cut, yellow rhinestones with a row of clear baguettes (decreasing in size toward the outer edge) running along each petal, and clear rhinestones in the folds of the petals. The oval-shaped corolla is covered with gray rhinestones. The earrings (not shown) are formed of two leaves in yellow and clear rhinestones.

NECKLACE WITH AURORA BOREALIS STONES

In contrast to Schiaparelli's mark in upper-case block letters, for which there is no official registration in the U.S. Patent Office in Washington, D.C., specific information about the mark in script affixed to this necklace can be found. In 1933 the Société Anonyme Schiaparelli, chaired by Elsa Schiaparelli, requested that this mark, which was used since 1927, be registered in the United States for clothing and accessories. The same mark had already been registered in France under the no. 278.023 in December 1931.

The body of the necklace consists of nine groups of stones. The cluster in the center, larger in size, is composed of eight prong-set Aurora Borealis stones, in varying shades of brown, either navette- or drop-cut. Smaller clusters of similar stones complete the necklace. The chain is silver plate.

Manufacturer
Unknown, for Elsa Schiaparelli

Place and Date of Manufacture
United States, late 1950s

Materials and Techniques
Partial silver-plated and partially burnished metal, crystal stones, Aurora Borealis stones

Mark
Schiaparelli

Provenance
Private collection

FESTOON NECKLACE

Manufacturer
Unknown, for Hattie
Canegie

**Place and Date
of Manufacture**
United States, late 1950s

**Materials and
Techniques**
Rhinestone chain,
plastic stones simulat-
ing Aurora Borealis,
rhinestones

Mark
Hattie Carnegie

Provenance
Private collection

Hattie Carnegie, born Henrietta Kanengeiser, still lingers in the memory of all but the youngest American women as the creator of the "little black dress," tight-waisted and rounded at the hips, and of palazzo pajamas for entertaining at home. Her models, taken from French haute couture at the beginning of her career in 1913 and then later on designed by her, are distinguished by quality fabrics and exceptional workmanship.

This festoon necklace was fashioned from iridescent plastic stones in azure and violet tones, mounted in groups with châton-cut rhinestones so as to form three triangular shapes with graduated corners. The chain and clasp are made of rhinestones. This is an effective example of the search for low-cost innovations: new at the time was the Aurora Borealis crystal stone, invented by Swarovski and launched on the international market by Dior; yet the plastic used here succeeds in creating a comparable effect at a much more moderate cost.

TRIFARI PARURE

TRIFARI

In the period from 1950–1960, after Mamie Eisenhower wore Trifari jewels to both of her husband's inaugural balls (1953 and 1957), Trifari's success was so great that it was necessary to offer a greater range of styles. As a result, so many designers were employed by Trifari, among them Jean Paris and André Boeuf, both from Cartier in Paris, that it is difficult to determine definitely that this parure was designed by Alfred Philippe. However, it is certainly true that this is an important set, worthy of the contemporary fashions that celebrated the recovery of peace and prosperity. The basic form of the necklace is composed of ten curvilinear, jointed segments in pavé-set rhinestones and oval fuchsia-colored glass stones. The central cluster, almost flowerlike, is thickly coated with fuchsia-colored faceted glass stones and more pavé-set rhinestones.

Designer
Probably Alfred Philippe

Manufacturer
Trifari, Krussman & Fishel, Inc.

Place and Date
of Manufacture
United States, late 1950s

Materials and
Techniques
Cast burnished metal, rhinestones, colored glass stones

Mark
Trifari

Provenance
Private collection, Milan

LARGE PECTORAL NECKLACE

Designer
Robert Clark

Manufacturer
Miriam Haskell Jewels

**Place and Date
of Manufacture**
New York, late 1950s
or early 1960s

**Materials and
Techniques**
Metal plates, *roses
montées*, faceted
crystal beads

Mark
Miriam Haskell

Provenance
Private collection,
New York

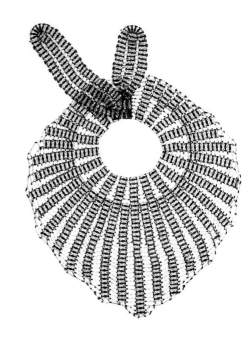

The shape of this necklace was inspired by a folded neckerchief draped across the décolletage and knotted in the back. It was made by mounting strips of increasing width, from the collar line outward, of alternating materials so as to yield one transparent stripe and one black one with a delicate addition of clear crystal. One of the stripes is formed of crystal beads that increase in number toward the outer edge of the necklace. The second stripe arises from small metal plates painted black, interspaced both above and below by rows of two or three transparent glass beads, each defined by two *roses montées*. The singularity of this necklace lies in its truly extraordinary size and in the refinement of its workmanship.

This necklace is very consistent with Haskell's style, but rather distant from the "sculptural" taste of its designer Robert Clark.

NECKLACE WITH
A CASCADE OF PEARLS

In the nonprecious ornament industry, revivals of styles of the past are recurrent. However, the examples most deserving of recognition are the intentional new editions that fall within the spirit of the current style of the period in which they come to pass.

For example, this beautiful example of a revival of the Edwardian style also captures the essence of fashion in the fifties, a decade of well-being that was signified by strapless evening gowns. The neck and the neckline became main focal points, and dog collars, simplified like this one and with more sober lines than in the past, were a perfect way of accentuating these features.

The necklace is composed of two parts: a collar and a long, double-strand pearl swag. The collar is three strands of simulated baroque pearls of slightly roseate glass with a stud clasp fashioned from gold-plated metal components, simulated pearls in a variety of sizes, and rhinestones. Two strands of simulated pearls, forming a teardrop-shaped design, descend from the clasp.

Manufacturer
Miriam Haskell Jewels

Place and Date of Manufacture
United States, late 1950s

Materials and Techniques
Glass simulated Baroque pearls, gold-plated metal components, glass-paste beads, small simulated pearls, rhinestones

Mark
Miriam Haskell

Provenance
Private collection

The Triumph of "Made in Italy":
1960–1969

COLLAR WITH NOSEGAYS
OF ROSES MONTÉES

Designer
Lyda Coppola

Manufacturer
Coppola & Toppo

**Place and Date
of Manufacture**
Milan, early 1960s

**Materials and
Techniques**
Crystals, synthetic
sponge balls, *roses
montées*, gold-plated
metal

Mark
Made in Italy by
Coppola & Toppo

Provenance
Private collection, Milan

Lyda Coppola's sojourn in Venice influenced her further development as a creator of costume jewelry. The traditions of forming and stringing beads, part of the cultural heritage of that city which has been handed down over the generations from artisan to artisan, emerged as part of Coppola's signature design work.

This collar necklace depicting imaginary flowers is composed of azure and blue crystals, which have been mounted on a base of sponge balls. Along the sides of the necklace, the crystals are interposed with nosegays of *roses montées* strung on a thin, silver-plated metal wire. The clasp, composed of crystals "sewn" on a metal gallery, has a gold-plated metal base and a chain that functions as an extender.

MADE IN ITALY
BY
Coppola Toppo

FESTOON NECKLACE WITH GOLD-PLATED METAL CIRCLES

Luciana's unusual genius enlivened the costume jewelry world beginning in the war years and then led to her even greater reputation in the coming years. In 1946 she created jewelry for Elizabeth Arden and Gucci; in 1950 she also began to export to the United States, thanks in part to her collaboration with Simonetta Visconti's atelier. Thus, Luciana became a successful interpreter of Italian style which over the course of the sixties became an international style, thanks especially to famous clients like Jacqueline Kennedy Onassis.

The necklace features seven festoons, graduated in size, hanging from chains attached to four trapezoid sections, interspaced with three châton stone settings. Each festoon is composed of one or more partially superimposed hand-cut circles of gold-plated, satinized metal decorated with three or four châton-cut, faceted crystal stones in yellow, violet, and green. Three more trapezoid plates occur on the sides of the necklace, connected to a chain and simple clasp.

Designer
Luciana Aloisi
De Reutern

Manufacturer
Luciana Aloisi
De Reutern

Place and Date of Manufacture
Italy, late 1960s

Materials and Techniques
Gold-plated satinized brass, crystal stones, chain

Mark
None

Provenance
Private collection

SERIES OF
NECKLACE CLASPS

Designer
Maria Vittoria Albani

Manufacturer
Ornella

**Place and Date
of Manufacture**
Milan, 1960–1969

**Materials and
Techniques**
Venetian-glass seed
beads, Venetian glass
beads, galvanized sea
shells and small snail
shells, gallery and base
in gold-plated metal
sheared and shaped
by hand

Mark
None

Provenance
Ornella Archives, Milan

What differentiates these necklaces from those usually seen in shops specializing in articles made from glass, especially in Venice, is the beauty and complexity of their clasps and their use of nontraditional stones such as the triple-fired, gold-plated ceramics. The skill in combining innovative materials with traditional stones characterizes jewelry produced by Ornella, a well-known brand throughout Europe, but especially in Germany where, since its inception, this company has found admirers and clients who have continued to buy its products year after year and collection after collection.

The clasp at left is composed of small snail shells that have been galvanized and arranged in the shape of corollas, with a stone of cobalt-blue glass paste in the center, and then sewn to an underlying gallery. The middle clasp consists of small sea shells glued to an underlying metal gallery and then galvanized. The clasp at right, a butterfly, was produced by sewing Venetian-glass seed beads to an underlying gallery and interposing them between drop-cut and châton stones.

DEMI-PARURE WITH SHELLS AND CORAL

The simplicity of humble materials (coral, shells, and cord) fits perfectly into the naturalistic, cheerful context of the hippie movement born in California in the middle of the sixties. The movement, an endorsement of nature and the environment, was symbolized by the peace symbol. Flower children were the so-called artisans of the period. Eventually costume jewelry manufacturers responded to this naturalistic philosophy, as seen here. This bracelet is composed of two strands of glass simulated pearls with a pendant formed from a large mother-of-pearl shell decorated at both ends with a small bunch of coral twigs. A thin braided cord supports a turquoise-colored glass-paste ball suspended from the shell. This same design is evident in the matching earrings.

Designer
Edoardo Borbonese

Manufacturer
Borbonese

Place and Date of Manufacture
Italy, late 1960s

Materials and Techniques
Glass simulated pearls, shell, cord, coral branches, turquoise-colored glass paste

Mark
Borbonese

Provenance
Borbonese Archive, Turin

Borbonese

PENDANT NECKLACE
OF METAL DISKS

Designer
Pietro Gentili

Manufacturer
Unknown, for
Germana Marucelli

**Place and Date
of Manufacture**
Milan, c. 1966

**Materials and
Techniques**
Silver-plated metal,
wire

Mark
P. Gentili

Provenance
Private collection

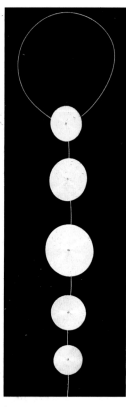

In the panorama of Italian fashion, Germana Marucelli is one of the personalities who is especially deserving of individual mention, not only as a stylist but as a promoter of young artists who, by special invitation, actively and directly participate in her creations. Marucelli is also remembered for her literary Thursdays, attended by poets Quasimodo and Montale as well as famous architects and intellectuals. From the sixties on, she has had sculptors and other artists working for her: Pietro Zuffi and Getulio Alviani design fabrics; Paolo Scheggi, Pietro Gentili, and Alviani create jewelry in both precious and nonprecious metals.

This collar necklace is fashioned from wire that is shaped into a ring. Five disks of hand-cut, silver-plated metal hang vertically. The disks grow from large to small, and each bears an engraved radial design.

P Gentili

RIGID NECKLACE
WITH PENDANT

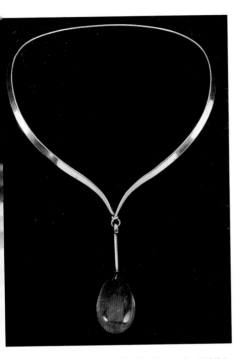

Designer
Torun Vivianna
Bülow-Hübe

Manufacturer
Torun Vivianna
Bülow-Hübe for
Georg Jensen

**Place and Date
of Manufacture**
Copenhagen, 1968

**Materials and
Techniques**
Cast silver, rock crystal

Mark
925 S Denmark Georg
Jensen Torun 169

Provenance
Private collection

Torun Vivianna Bülow-Hübe, born in 1927 in Sweden, won the silver medal at the tenth Milan Triennial in 1954 and the gold medal at the twelfth Triennial in 1960. In 1965 she was awarded the Grand Prix of Sweden. This rigid necklace with a rosy-colored rock crystal embodies Torun's vision of the ideal ornament: "The jewel must be married to the contours of a woman's body. In a word, it must be sensual."

The necklace beautifully displays the geometric essence of Danish design that was abundantly influenced by creators like Jensen and Magnusen. Torun is a magnificent interpreter of this Danish style as she continues along the paths of a tradition that has made a name for itself at the international level.

FLOWER BROOCH
IN TONES OF VIOLET AND LILAC

Designer
Cissy Zoltowska

Manufacturer
Cissy Zoltowska

**Place and Date
of Manufacture**
France, early 1960s

**Materials and
Techniques**
Silver-plated metal
components, glass
stones, leaves in
stamped glass paste

Mark
None

Provenance
Francine Cohen
Collection, New Jersey

In the *Corriere di informazione* for January
27–28, 1962, Irene Brin offered a bit of news
that revealed the "noble" levels that costume
jewelry had attained in those years. She wrote
in shorthand style: "...Cocktail party for Cis
jewelry, and a revelation about the tiara that
Princess Paola of Liège wore to the *Bal des
petits lits blancs*. An Indian tiara, matching her
Indian-style gown designed for her by Lanvin-
Castillo, and one that you might have thought
was on special loan from the court treasury.
But no, it was from Cis, the most majestic fake
in the world."

This brooch was fashioned from silver-
plated metal, soldered to a central bar supporting the clasp for the brooch and ending in settings of different shapes and sizes. The stones,
in shades of violet and lilac, are mainly châton-
cut in a variety of large and medium sizes, interspaced with violet cabochons. Two leaves
in stamped green glass complete the corolla.

COLLAR WITH RED FISH AND GREEN POLYPS

Monique Vedié, born in 1924, was already interested in costume jewelry while she was attending the School of Applied Arts in Paris. Her encounter with Victor Linton, a creator of jewelry made from cellulose acetate, was a decisive moment in her career. This synthesized material was discovered by chance and became popular because of the scarcity of metal materials during the war years. When Linton decided to retire in 1948, Vedié took over his atelier at 52 rue de Richelieu where she created her first pieces of costume jewelry: hat pins, earrings, and scarf pins. Naturally, her favorite material was acetate and her themes were taken from nature: fish, birds, feathers, and flowers. In 1976 she moved to 1 rue Mehul, where she worked until her retirement in 1992.

This necklace is formed of a strand of cylindrical stems of green glass paste on which are strung, at regular intervals, three red fish, two green polyps, and five spacers fashioned by taking a segment of round gilded acetate, winding it into three loops, and folding one end of the segment over the other. The screw clasp is gold-plated metal.

Designer
Monique Vedié

Manufacturer
Monique Vedié

Place and Date of Manufacture
France, early 1960s

Materials and Techniques
Cellulose acetate, bored green glass-paste tubes, gold-plated metal

Mark
None

Provenance
Private collection

DUAL-PURPOSE TIE BROOCH

Designer
Jacques Gautier
Manufacturer
Jacques Gautier
Place and Date of Manufacture
France, late 1960s
Materials and Techniques
Handworked metal, stamped-metal chain, crystal and enamel stones
Mark
None
Provenance
Maxela Collection, Milan

Jacques Gautier, a young artist at heart, began his career in the theater which he later abandoned to undergo a period of apprenticeship with François Hugo, a well-known master glass-maker. Gautier took an interest in ancient Venetian techniques and decided to apply them in creating costume jewelry for haute couture. In 1948 Christian Dior, who had admired Gautier's geometric ornaments in crystal and colored enamel, adapted them for his clothing. Their collaboration continued, even though Gautier was also working for Rochas, Fath, and Lelong at the time. In 1958 Gautier opened a boutique at 36 rue Jacob that is still in operation.

This brooch is composed of two plates of hammered metal inset with crystal inserts on an enameled base. The plates are connected by a long chain made of stamped metal with a finely hatched surface. When pinned to the center of the neckline, the brooch is transformed into a unisex necklace, which was also very popular with male customers in the late 1960s.

BROOCH WITH IMAGINARY FLOWERS

During the sixties, rather than being mere adornments, ornaments became an attribute of the outfit whose fabrics, colors, and shapes were part of a theme to which the accessories were also tied in order to create a total look.

Madame Gripoix did not remember which collection this brooch was conceived for. We would like to think of it as paired with one of Saint-Laurent's neutral-colored suits, perhaps even with one of his bush jackets. These jackets, as well as the designer's tuxedos, made history by abolishing, in effect, the sharp boundary between men's and women's clothing.

The brooch depicts two imaginary flowers resting on a stem with stylized leaves, both executed in glass paste with a gold-plated metal border. The flower in the foreground has a corolla formed of a gold-plated metal pistil in the shape of a sun with a black-paste cabochon in the center. The pistil is encircled by seven petals of yellow glass paste painted with black spots, and interspaced with seven other petals in white. Behind it is a flower with an azure glass-paste pistil encircled by four petals of the same color, interspaced with five others in bright azure glass paste. A long stem with small bunches of stylized leaves, formed from green glass paste, supports the two corollas.

Designer
Josette Gripoix
Manufacturer
Gripoix for Yves Saint-Laurent
Place and Date of Manufacture
France, c. 1967
Materials and Techniques
Glass paste, gold-plated metal
Mark
None
Provenance
Lo Scrigno del Tempo Collection

COLLAR WITH
STRASS FLOWERS

Manufacturer
Henkel & Grosse

**Place and Date
of Manufacture**
Pforzheim (Germany),
1966

Materials and Techniques
Stamped glass pastes,
Aurora Borealis stones,
silver-plated metal
components

Mark
C. Dior 1966

Provenance
Private collection

In this necklace, elegant and sumptuous enough for a movie star (originally made for Sophia Loren), the way in which the stones were mounted enhances the brilliance of the stones and the overall freshness of the leaves and flowers. The mounting in front is nearly invisible, so that the Aurora Borealis stones look like a dazzling bouquet of flowers. In all, nine different flowers have been fashioned from the Aurora Borealis strass. The back of the necklace is composed of stamped green glass leaves.

BROOCH IN THE SHAPE
OF A SHOOT

A designer and manufacturer of costume jewelry, Max Müller was born in Jablonec Nad Nisou in Bohemia, where he attended the Kunstgewerbliche Staatsfachschule. Later on in Vienna, he also attended the Wiener Werkstätte.

In 1946 in Kaufbeuren in Bavaria, he set up his own business which made a name for itself as a manufacturer of fashion ornaments inspired by ancient models. In the sixties and the seventies, Müller worked for the movies and the theater and numbered among his clients the actresses Sophia Loren and Marlene Dietrich, as well as many other movie stars of the time.

His jewelry is characterized by a varied use of wire and both colored and transparent blown glass. In 1987 his business was turned over to Wilhelm Kemp. A few ornaments that are representative of Max Müller's entire line of production can be seen at the Museum of Kaufbeuren in Neugablonz, Germany.

This brooch depicts a branch fashioned from a sinuous piece of wire with five large burnt-orange leaves in acrylic that have been stamped to create the veining effect. Part of the shoot is covered with stones of clear baguette-cut glass that were also used to form the petals of the flowers. The pistils are either glass simulated pearl or a châton rhinestone.

Designer
Max Müller

Manufacturer
Max Müller

**Place and Date
of Manufacture**
Kaufbeuren-
Neugablonz
(Germany), c. 1966

**Materials and
Techniques**
Gold-plated wire,
rhinestones, glass
simulated pearls,
stamped acrylic

Mark
Max Müller

Provenance
Private collection

CROSS-SHAPED PLEXIGLAS BROOCH

Designer
Stanley Hagler

Manufacturer
Stanley Hagler

**Place and Date
of Manufacture**
United States, late 1960s

**Materials and
Techniques**
Plexiglas, rhinestones,
stamped gold-plated
metal components

Mark
Stanley Hagler, N.Y.C.

Provenance
Private collection

After graduating from the University of Denver
with a degree in law, in 1951 Stanley Hagler
began to devote himself to costume jewelry,
setting up a small workshop in New York's
Greenwich Village. In 1968, having reached the
heights of success with his multipurpose jewelry, dramatic and extreme in its architectural
structure, Hagler received one of the prizes
attached to the "Great Designs in Costume
Jewelry" program. His remarks, recorded in an
article reporting on the prize, give the best interpretation of his style: "The point of creating
exaggerated objects is that in order to be successful, you must underline your own point of
view. If the average necklace reaches the middle of the bust, bring yours down to the navel.
You certainly won't look like the average
woman. It is an extreme fashion, which, when
it reaces its highest point, establishes a trend."

The crosses of the brooch are equal-sized
triangular, faceted plexiglas. The central area,
a four-lobed design in gold-plated metal
stamped to simulate filigree, is further decorated with rhinestones.

FESTOON NECKLACE

Mimi di Niscemi, cousin of Fulco di Verdura and a graduate of the Philadelphia Museum School, also attended the School of Applied Arts in Paris. In 1962 she set up her own company, Mimi di N., in New York. Not only did she design and produce costume jewelry, she developed an archive of designs. In a few short years her creations appeared in all the important fashion magazines. This festoon necklace displays three clusters of stones that are surrounded by cabochons and navette-cut crystals.

Designer
Mimi di Niscemi

Manufacturer
Mimi di Niscemi

Place and Date
of Manufacture
United States, mid-1960s

Materials and Techniques
Silver-plated metal, plastic, crystal and glass-paste stones

Mark
Mimi di N.

Provenance
Private collection

COLLAR IN GOLD-PLATED
SATINIZED METAL

Manufacturer
Joseph Mazer
& Co., Inc.

**Place and Date
of Manufacture**
United States, late 1960s

**Materials and
Techniques**
Cast gold-plated
metal, crystal stones,
rhinestones

Mark
Jomaz

Provenance
Private collection

In the period from 1950 to 1963, Jomaz signified costume jewelry whose traditional design derived from fine jewelry making. Although the Jomaz name was never registered at the U.S. Patent Office in Washington, D.C., it was used by the Joseph Mazer Company, Inc., of New York as a conflation of their name. The company had been founded by Joseph Mazer and his brother, Louis, in 1926 as Mazer Bros. In 1927 they went their separate ways, with Joseph now calling the business Joseph J. Mazer Co., specializing in precious stones. By 1948 it was listed as a manufacturer of costume jewelry. Mazer jewelry shows its fine heritage.

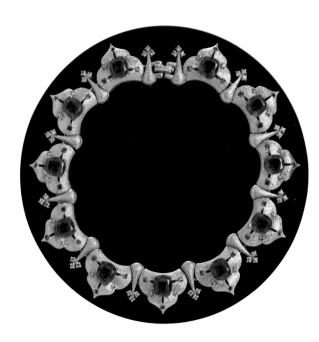

EARRINGS WITH OCTAGONAL PENDANT

Manufacturer
Kenneth Jay Lane

Place and Date of Manufacture
New York, late 1960s

Materials and Techniques
Glass paste, rhinestones, burnished metal components

Mark
K.J.L.

Provenance
Private collection, Milan

The traits that distinguish Kenneth Jay Lane are his canny skills and aesthetic "eye" for copying important jewels of great value. This does not mean that he is not extremely clever at devising original jewelry. But the reason for his fame is certainly tied to his ability to intuit that costume jewelry copies of historically acclaimed jewels are gestures of the utmost irony and therefore of a critical intelligence. And so the famous Webb bracelets, Bulgari necklaces, and Cartier pins became, with Kenneth Lane, nonprecious ornaments whose magnificence remained extremely beautiful.

These hanging earrings are of burnished metal, each one having a fastener formed with a coral-colored glass-paste drop, surrounded by a ring of rhinestones. The drop supports a circular design of eight fuchsia-colored glass-paste stones in a rounded rectangular cut, alternated with a series of small circular cabochons in coral-colored glass paste.

In the center is a round cabochon in the same coral-colored glass paste, and encircled by small transparent rhinestones is the eye-catching center of the earring.

K.J.L.

COLLAR OF PEARLIZED
BLOWN-GLASS SPHERES

Manufacturer
Brania

**Place and Date
of Manufacture**
United States, late
1960s

**Materials and
Techniques**
Pearlized blown-glass
spheres, gold-plated
metal, rhinestones

Mark
Brania

Provenance
Carolle Thibaut-
Pomerantz Collection,
Paris

Brania is one of the many firms headquartered in New York that distribute costume jewelry created at the request of contractors who make jewelry to order, but remain anonymous as the objects fashioned by them take on the trademark of the company that ordered them. The Brania brand is mostly known for simulated-pearl jewelry and ornaments made from glass which tend to be highly exaggerated or dramatic and come in unusual sizes. Mimi di Niscemi worked for them in the early sixties and probably left an indelible impression on their style, which was nevertheless very much in harmony with the sixties when the whole of fashion, before the turning-point year of 1968, was pomp, luxury, exaggeration, and ostentation. This necklace, with a presence conferred by the extraordinary dimensions of its simulated pearls that was perfect for those years, is composed of twelve pearlized blown-glass spheres on a gold-plated stamped-metal base and spaced with eleven rhinestones.

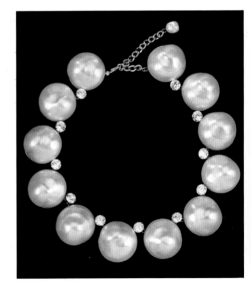

DAISY-SHAPED PINS

As had never before occurred, fashion in the sixties took two different roads: professionals in the field saw a woman as a goddess to be dressed up in gold, silks, damasks, furs, wigs, and so on; on the other hand, young people saved their energies for existential, philosophical, and political problems, and dressed in conformity with their new ideals. Pacifists, feminists, and those who sympathized with the civil rights movement and other progressive movements wanted to identify themselves by simple, almost monastic clothing and by the symbols that they displayed on their bodies in the form of tattoos or ornaments dangling from leather or rope thongs. Therefore, many costume jewelry manufacturers made floral pins, earrings, and necklaces similar to this group of brightly colored pins in an attempt to attract an ever-increasing market: "flower children."

Place and Date of Manufacture
United States, late 1960s

Materials and Techniques
Stamped and fire-enameled metal

Mark
None

Provenance
Private collection

PRODUCERS AND MANUFACTURERS

Andersen, David, Oslo
The David Andersen firm was founded in Oslo in 1876. Their production, associated with colored enamels, continues until this day. Cf. p. 198.

Balle, Norway
There is no detailed information on this designer who operated in Norway in the 1950s and 60s. It is likely the business no longer exists. Cf. p. 200.

Baretti, Lina, Paris
A creator of *bijoux de couture*, made entirely by hand with unusual materials (velvet, tinsel, and trimmings), Baretti was active in Paris, especially in the 1950s and 60s.

Bengel, Jakob, Idar Oberstein, Germany
A manufacturer of watch chains from 1871 on, and subsequently, from 1930 on, a manufacturer of costume jewelry in galalith and chrome, Bengel mostly exported to the United States and France. The business closed in 1933. Cf. p. 82.

Bliss, E. A., Co., North Attleboro, Massachusetts, and Meriden, Connecticut
Founded in North Attleboro, Massachusetts in 1875 when E. A. Bliss took over the Whitney Rice Co., in 1893 the firm began to produce gift articles and ornaments in silver. In 1922 the firm's name was changed to the Napier Co., after its then president. Napier still exists today. Cf. pp. 92, 94.

Block, Fred A., Chicago
A producer of articles of clothing for women since 1933, it was probably the same firm that distributed costume jewelry signed Fred A. Block Jewelry. It dates from the mid-1930s up to the end of the 1950s, when the firm probably closed. Cf. p. 142.

Bonaz, Auguste, Oyonnax, France
Precise historical references surround the firm of Auguste Bonaz with fame. The business was founded by César Bonaz, the man charged by his fellow citizens with the task of making a precious comb of engraved horn to be presented to Empress Eugénie on the occasion of her visit to Oyonnax with Napoleon III. César's son, Auguste, broadened the activities of the firm and earned international success producing costume jewelry, ornaments for the hair, cases, and toilet articles with a simple, linear, geometric style. Auguste died in 1922, and the firm was successfully carried on by his wife, Marie Bailly, who was already in charge of the Paris branch at 7 rue de Metz. Madame Bonaz passed away in 1927, and the running of the business passed to her grandson, Theo Bailly, who remained as head of the firm until it closed in 1982. Cf. pp. 76, 77, 152.

Bonté, Elisabeth, France
Her activities as a designer and maker of horn jewelry, especially pendants, made her famous in the early decades of the 20th century. Bonté's workshop was absorbed by Georges Pierre (signature GIP), her chief rival in the manufacturing of horn jewelry. Elisabeth Bonté worked with Georges Pierre until the mid-1930s.

Borbonese, Turin
Sometime around the mid-1930s, Luciana Borbonese took over a shop that sold costume jewelry and trimmings for dresses and turned it into a thriving business headquartered at 9 Via Bogino. Her products were greatly influenced by the designs of Turin's great couturiers. Distribution of her jewelry, originally limited to Turin, was broadened to include the rest of Italy and France in the 1960s. Currently their production has stabilized at a few thousand pieces per year, each one skillfully worked by hand. Cf. p. 223.

Boucher, Marcel & Cie, New York
After having worked as an apprentice for Cartier, Marcel Boucher emigrated to the United States in the early 1920s. By the mid-1930s, Saks Fifth Avenue featured a set of his brooches based on the theme of birds, thus initiating the firm's reputation as a creator of costume jewelry. The firm was quite successful until it closed down in 1971. Cf. pp. 148, 212.

Bozart, Milan
Originating as a small craftsmen's enterprise managed by Emy and Giuseppe Manca, over the course of the 1960s the firm produced more than 8,000 pieces a year for the most important Italian designers. In the 1970s Bozart collaborated with Barocco,

Lancetti, and **Balestra**. Since 1982, the running of the firm has been entrusted to the founders' son, Maurizio Manca. Cf. p. 192.

Brania, New York
A distributor of costume jewelry made by "contractors." Cf. p. 236.

Calderoni, Milan
Calderoni produces and distributes costume jewelry and other objects in silver. It was founded in 1840 and continues today as Calderoni Gioielli Spa. Cf. p. 160.

Carnegie, Hattie, New York
Hattie Carnegie, known for the "little Carnegie dress"—tight-waisted and with defined hips—dressed American women of the beau monde as well as stars of the stage and screen, among them Constance Bennet and Joan Crawford. The firm that created costume jewelry with the Hattie Carnegie mark was sold to Paristyle Holding, Ltd. of New York in the mid-1980s. Cf p. 214.

Ciner Manufacturing Co., New York
Ciner Manufacturing Co., founded in 1892 in New York, is still in operation. Cf. p. 149.

C. I. S. (Cissy Zoltowska), Paris
For the last few years, Cissy Zoltowska has been living in California where she continues her activity as a costume jewelry designer, but at a more modest level. Cf. pp. 175, 226.

Cohn & Rosenberger (Coro Inc. from 1943 on), New York
Cohn & Rosenberger, founded in 1901, which became Coro Inc. in 1943, was the first costume jewelry producer to be quoted on the stock exchange. At present, the firm operates exclusively in Canada. Cf. p. 138.

Coppola & Toppo, Milan
Lyda Coppola's mixed background—her mother was from Trieste, her father from Turin, and her ancestors were Neapolitans—may perhaps be responsible for the commingling of styles in costume jewelry by this sensitive artist. Her production is characterized by unusual combinations of typically Italian materials from different areas of the peninsula, such as Venetian glass and coral from Torre del Greco. After studying at the Academia di Belle Arti in Venice, she moved to Milan where Ada Politzer guided her in the rudiments of the art of costume jewelry. In 1948 Lyda Coppola made her professional debut in Paris with her jewelry created for Fath and Schiaparelli. The firm of Coppola & Toppo shut down in 1986, a few years after Lyda Coppola's death. Cf. pp. 162, 163, 186, 220.

David, Etienne, Paris
We have no information regarding this jeweler, who worked on the rue de la Paix in Paris in the 1920s and 30s, other than that cited on page 71, which was taken from Roulet's *Bijoux Art Déco*, published by Editions du Regard in 1984.

De Rosa, Ralph, Co., New York
The Ralph De Rosa firm was run by three women of Italian descent (Elvira, the designer, Virginia, the president, and Theresa) and operated in New York from 1935 to 1955. De Rosa jewels exemplify what we now call retro jewelry—showy and opulent, but nonetheless harmonious and suitable for the kind of woman who is sure enough of herself to be a little daring, even in her choice of jewelry. Cf. p. 142.

Di Niscemi, Mimi, New York
In 1968 Mimi di Niscemi won one of the thirty-five prizes offered by the Great Designs in Costume Jewelry Awards program, sponsored by D. Swavorski & Co. Cf. p. 233.

Du Jay, New York
The Du Jay firm acted as a wholesaler of both real and costume jewelry. Only rarely can pieces of costume jewelry signed Du Jay be found in the antiques market. Cf. p. 121.

Eisenberg & Sons, Chicago
Jewelry from the 1930s, 40s, and 50s signed with one of Eisenberg's marks (E, Eisenberg, Eisenberg Original) can be recognized by the consistently very high quality of the stones, by their hand settings, and by the metals employed: sterling silver or an alloy that resembles pewter. Cf. p. 147.

Fahrner, Theodor, Pforzheim, Germany
Theodor Fahrner, a producer of precious and semiprecious jewelry, was one of the few non-French firms that attained international success at the beginning of this century. Cf. pp. 66, 81, 164.

Fishel, Nessler & Co., New York
The notes about this firm recorded on page 95 were taken from Dorothy Rainwater's *American Jewelry Manufactur-*

ers, published by Schiffer in 1988.

Flamand, Paris
This firm, a manufacturer of costume jewelry known especially for its baubles made from Bakelite or horn, appears to have been in operation from the end of the 19th century until about 1980. Its offices were on the rue Turbigo in Paris. Cf. p. 109.

Fratti, Giuliano, Milan
Giuliano Fratti is Italy's only *parurier*. In fact, his production extended to encompass all kinds of clothing supplies and accessories (belts, buttons, trimmings, ornaments for the hair, and costume jewelry). Cf. pp. 158, 188.

Furla, Bologna
The Furla company had its antecedents in a small enterprise, founded in 1928 by Aldo Furlanetto, that distributed articles for haberdashery, leather goods, and costume jewelry. Today, through the commitment and passion of Furlanetto's sons, the firm specializes in leather goods and accessories as a direct distributor at the national and international level. Cf. p. 191.

Gablonzer Genossenschaft, Gablonzer, Austria
The products of the Gablonzer Genossenschaft (cooperative) are indicative of the exceptional quality and workmanship that mark costume jewelry produced in Austria. This country has a time-honored tradition of manufacturing jewelry for the fashion industry and is famous for its inventive designers and for the beauty of the stones used in its jewelry.

Gautier, Jacques, Paris
This creator's period of greatest success was at the end of the 1960s, when the unisex style allowed even men to wear ornaments. His mastery of glassworking techniques also made it possible for him to create the stained-glass windows for the church in Grimaud. Cf. p. 228.

GIP (see **Pierre, Georges**)

Glass, Leo & Company, Inc., New York
Notes relating to this firm, in operation in New York from 1943 to 1957, can be found on page 202.

Goosens, Robert, Paris
Since 1958, Robert Goosens has created much of the jewelry signed Balenciaga. At present, he collaborates with Yves Saint-Laurent, Dior, Sonia Rykiel, and Kenzo, creating both costume jewelry and other objects such as cases and perfume bottles. Cf. p. 185.

Gripoix, Paris
Costume jewelry executed by Gripoix (unsigned except for the inscription *France* or *Deposé*) is very highly sought-after in the period-jewelry market. The firm is currently managed by Josette Gripoix's son Thierry. Cf. pp. 171, 173, 176, 178, 229.

Hagler, Stanley, New York
At present, Stanley Hagler lives in Florida and continues, at a more modest level of activity, to make costume jewelry that recalls the styles of his work in the 1960s and 1970s. Cf. p. 232.

Henkel & Grosse, Pforzheim, Germany
Founded in 1907 by Heinrich Henkel and Florentin Grosse, after the First World War the firm devoted itself to manufacturing costume jewelry for the European market, and towards the end of the 1920s, for the American market as well. In 1937 Henkel & Grosse received the certificate of honor at the Paris Exposition. Cf. pp. 182, 183, 184, 230.

Hobé, New York
The firm is still in operation in New York and has set up a small museum of objects produced by the company in the past. The museum, located in the company's showroom, is open to the public. Cf. p. 139.

Horner, Charles, Halifax, England
Charles Horner was one of the most important firms in England in the field of semiprecious jewelry, in particular for its hat pins, and because, at the beginning of this century, it was the first company to mechanize its manufacturing processes. Cf. p. 67.

Jensen, Georg, Copenhagen
The son of a foundryman, Georg Jensen worked as an apprentice to a silversmith and later attended a vocational school for artisans. He received a diploma from the Royal Academy of Fine Arts in Copenhagen and showed in the 1900 Paris Exposition as a potter. In 1902 he began to design jewelry in Mogen Ballin's workshop. In 1904 he opened his own workshop, and by 1909 he already had a branch in Berlin which was then followed by other branches in London, Paris, and Barcelona. The jewelry he produced in the

early years of this century, executed in silver with an extensive use of semi-precious materials (amber, chalcedony, carnelian, agate) are now being replicated and sold in Georg Jensen stores all over the world. Cf. p. 225

Joseff of Hollywood, Inc., Burbank, California

At present, Joseff of Hollywood is managed by Joan Castle Joseff (the wife of the firm's founder, Eugene Joseff) who continues to reissue the original models, each of which was preserved because the jewels were intended to be rented to movie studios rather than to be sold. Cf. pp. 127, 136.

Kleiss, H., Austria

There is no specific information about this creator who worked in Austria in the 1930s. Cf. p. 87.

Kollmar & Jourdan, Pforzheim, Germany

For information about this firm see page 80.

Kunstgewerbeschule, Vienna

This Viennese art school was established in 1867, and in 1903 its teachers founded the Wiener Werkstätte. Cf. p. 63.

Lane, Kenneth Jay, New York

The firm of Kenneth Jay Lane is headquartered in New York and directly distributes its costume jewelry at numerous points of sale, including London, Paris, and of course, New York. Cf. p. 235.

Luciana (Aloisi de Reutern), Rome

Luciana (Aloisi de Reutern) also devoted herself to the creation of real jewelry and objects for the home. She closed her business in 1983. Cf. pp. 189, 221.

Mazer Bros., New York

Mazer Bros. began a jewelry business in 1917 in Philadelphia. Then in 1926 they moved to New York and in 1939 they started to produce costume jewelry, all with hand-set rhinestones. Mazer Bros. was known for its innovative design and production methods. Marcel Boucher was one of their designers and André Fleurides, who came from Van Cleef & Arpels, worked with them from 1940 through the postwar period. In 1946 Louis and Joseph Mazer separated and Joseph operated his own business, known by the name of his trademark, JOMAZ. Louis continued with Mazer Bros. until 1951. Cf. p. 234.

Miriam Haskell Jewels, New York

Miriam Haskell, owned since 1989 by Frank Fialkoff, is still in operation, reissuing the classic models of the original Haskell. Cf. pp. 144, 145, 146, 208, 209, 210, 211, 216, 217.

Napier (see **Bliss, E. A., Co.**)

Ornella, Milan

From 1946 on, Maria Vittoria Albani, Ornella's current proprietor, assisted her mother Piera Barni in running this small firm specializing in handmade costume jewelry, in particular necklaces. The firm, originally located in Piazza Piola, has been on the Via Carducci since the mid-1950s. As in the past, the firm continues to produce handmade, feminine jewelry with a characteristic timeless quality. Cf. pp. 161, 190, 222.

Pellini Caimi, Emma, Milan

At present, Pellini jewelry, designed by Donatella Pellini who is the granddaughter of the firm's founder and who also supervises production, is sold directly in Milan and through exclusive distributors in major cities throughout the world. Cf. p. 187.

Pennino Bros., New York

Pennino jewels are stamped and can be easily identified by their naturalistic subjects rendered with grace and elegance. Information about this firm can be found on page 143.

Péral, Jeanne, Paris

The most recurrent materials in Jeanne Péral's *bijoux de couture* are rhinestones, Swarovski stones, enamels, ivory, horn, wood, coral, and amberlite (a plastic that simulates amber). The sources of her inspiration are found in nature and in the art of many countries. Cf. p. 181.

Perli, Schwäbisch Gmünd, Germany

The Pe stamp, which appears on costume jewelry produced by this firm, is so small that it frequently passes unobserved. Information about this producer can be found on page 195.

Peruzzi Jewel Shop, Boston

The preferred subjects for ornaments produced by this firm are almost always taken from mythology as well as Roman, Etruscan, and Greek archeological finds. Further information can be found on page 207.

Pfeiffer, Juliane, Sweden

We have no information on this designer other than the fact that she worked for a jeweler named Bolin in the 1950s. Cf. p. 199.

Piel Frères (later Paul Piel & Fils), *Paris*
This firm, which started in Paris in the latter half of the 19th century and became Paul Piel & Fils in 1920, was one of the first to dedicate itself entirely to the production of humble jewelry in which celluloid takes the place of ivory, and copper and silver replace gold. Cf. pp. 52, 53.

Pierre, Georges (GIP), French Jura
Specializing in handworked horn jewelry, Georges Pierre carried out his activities in French Jura from the end of the 19th century until 1930. He then took over the workshop of Elisabeth Bonté, his rival in the making of horn jewelry, especially pendants, and worked with her until 1936. Cf. p. 54.

Prusac, Lola, Paris
Information about this creator, whose boutique is still in operation in Paris, can be found on page 180.

Rebajes, Francisco, New York
Information about this creator, who retired to Torremolinos, Spain in the early 1960s after closing down his operation in New York, can be found on page 204.

Renoir of California, Los Angeles
Founded by Jerry Fels in 1946 and headquartered in Los Angeles, this firm specialized in the manufacture of costume jewelry in copper (stamped Renoir) and fire-enameled copper (stamped Renoir/Matisse), with a linear geometric design sometimes inspired by primitive art. At the beginning of the 1960s, when the fashion for A-line dresses required elaborate jewelry to alleviate the naked, unadorned lines of the clothing, Renoir's popularity declined and the firm finally went out of business in 1964. Cf. p. 201.

Rivière, Madeleine, Paris
Information about this firm can be found on pages 170 and 177.

Rousselet, Louis, Paris
Notes about this firm can be found on page 115. Jewels produced by the firm are reproduced on pages 155 and 172.

Sandor, New York
Information relating to this firm, which specialized in enameled costume jewelry with naturalistic subjects, can be found on page 137.

Simpson, Adele, New York
This privately owned firm was founded in 1949 and still exists today. Simpson dressed three generations of First Ladies, from Lady Bird Johnson to Pat Nixon and Barbara Bush. The key to this firm's success probably lies in the fact that clothing and jewelry signed Adele Simpson are still, and always will be, "wearable." Cf. p. 206.

Staret, Chicago
The style and sometimes excessively showy shapes of costume jewelry stamped Staret recall the more famous jewels of Eisenberg & Sons. Staret operated in Chicago from 1941 to 1947. Cf. p. 93.

Tostrup, J., Oslo
This firm was founded around 1838 by Jacob Tostrup, who became a master goldsmith in 1852. A manufacturer of flatware and hollowware and, starting from the 20th century, silver jewelry, the firm has won several international awards for the excellence of its work. It was influential in the 19th century revival of filigree work and enamels, especially *plique à jour* and *champlevé*. Cf. p. 197.

Trifari, Krussman & Fishel, New York
The Trifari family, originally from Naples, was engaged in jewelry production by the mid-19th century. The gloomy economic conditions of the early 20th century prompted one member of the family, Augusto Trifari, to emigrate to the United States. In 1909, after a long apprenticeship with a jeweler, he set up a facility for producing costume jewelry under the name Trifari. After a number of changes, Trifari, Krussman & Fishel, named after the partners who ran the business, was finally established in 1925. In 1930 Alfred Philippe, who had previously worked for William Scheer, a company that produced jewelry for Cartier, entered the firm as chief designer. Trifari jewelry became overwhelmingly popular and the national advertising campaigns that began in 1938 further reinforced their success. At present, after a series of changes in ownership, Trifari continues to produce low-cost costume jewelry. Cf. pp. 105, 140, 203, 215.

Vedié, Monique, Paris
This creator's favorite material, acetate, is pyrographed and then covered with metal, cloth, or rhinestones, with unprecedented results. Vedié worked with Lanvin, Dior, and Ungaro. Cf. p. 227.

GLOSSARY

À jour (said of enamel) Open-work setting which allows for the passage of light.

Acetate Thermoplastic resin derived from formaldehyde. Has a crystalline appearance and excellent mechanical properties.

Acrylic resin A derivative of acrylic acid, it is a thermoplastic substance of exceptional transparency, luster, and great industrial strength.

Agate A semiprecious hard stone belonging to the chalcedony family, translucent and with concentric layers. It can be easily dyed and worked.

Amazonite A mineral in the feldspar family, with a light green color.

Amber A natural material (fossil resin of coniferous plants) with a yellow-red color. Today there are excellent imitations of amber; when rubbed, true amber attracts paper.

Amethyst A mineral belonging to the quartz family, with a transparent violet color.

Amine A basic organic compound derived from ammonia that is used for manufacturing synthetic resins of various kinds.

Amulet An object believed to be capable of guarding against misfortune and danger because of its shape and substance.

Antiqued In reference to metal, it means aged, such as antiqued gold-plating or silver-plating.

Antiqued gilding Gold-plating on copper without subsequent polishing.

Artist's jewelry A piece of jewelry (in precious, semiprecious, or humble materials) made by a painter or sculptor and usually produced in a limited number of copies.

Aurora Borealis Faceted glass stones with an iridescent color.

Aventurine A variety of microcrystalline quartz whose yellowish green color comes from inclusions of various types of minerals.

Bakelite The first entirely synthetic resin belonging to the phenolic resin class, patented in 1909 by Leo Baekeland, a Belgian chemist residing in the United States. It was especially popular in the period between the two world wars.

Bandeau (Fr.) A band worn across the forehead, generally with small woven beads, suitable for holding the hair in place. Especially popular between 1920 and 1930.

Baroque pearl A real or simulated pearl with an irregular shape.

Basse taille (Fr.) An enameling technique that involves a process such as chasing or stamping a metal background, then fusing to it a layer of translucent or transparent enamel. The result is similar to intaglio relief.

Bayadère (Fr.) A multistrand necklace of seed pearls, about 46 cm. in length.

Beaded A surface decorated with small beads resembling fresh-water pearls. When this type of ornamentation is very small, the surface is said to be "granulated."

Bijoutier faussetier (Fr. for counterfeit jeweler) One who makes copies of real jewels in common or semiprecious metals (for example silver). The association for this category of producers was founded in Paris in 1873 under the presidency of Alexander Piel.

Bijou de couture (Fr.) An ornament created from nonprecious materials, generally handmade and in a limited number of copies, conceived by couturiers for their high fashion clothing. Originating in France with the birth of haute couture around 1910, this jewelry made a name for itself in the 1920s and 30s, thanks to Coco Chanel and Elsa Schiaparelli, and then spread to the rest of Europe and to America. The *bijou de couture* reflects the specific style of the couturier who paired it with one of his or her outfits and is changed over the course of the designer's collections.

Bracelet Ornament for the wrist and the arms. Various types exist:
>   **bangle** (ring-shaped in metal, plastic, or wood; it can be smooth, faceted, decorated, or set with stones)
>   **charm** (a chain bracelet with hanging charms)
>   **cuff** (a nonflexible bracelet, usually wide)

hinged (partially rigid or jointed with a mechanism for opening and closing)

link or *flexible* (made up of metal units linked to one another)

slave (worn on the upper arm)

spiral (two or three circlets of simulated pearls or glass beads strung on a harmonic wire).

Brass Metal alloy containing 65% copper and 33% zinc.

Brilliant cut Type of cut used for almost all diamonds, to the degree that "brilliant" commonly means a diamond cut with a rounded shape and 56 facets.

Brooch An ornament with a pin clasp in an infinite variety of shapes, materials, and sizes, used as a decoration for the bust. There are a variety of types of brooches:

bar brooch (composed of an oblong fastening from which a pendant is suspended)

chatelaine (two brooches connected by a chain or a single brooch with chains gathered together to form a hanging ornament)

fob (a brooch consisting of a fastener and a hanging, movable, decorative element)

plaque brooch (flat ornament with a rectangular or square shape)

stick pin (an ornament composed of a decorative motif at one end of a pin and protected at the other end by a safety cap to both fasten the pin and keep the pin from pricking the wearer)

tremblant (a brooch, generally in the shape of a flower, with a unit attached to a spring that moves with the wearer)

Burin Steel implement similar to a thin chisel, used to engrave metals by hand.

Burnish Treatment of metal surfaces to darken them.

Cabochon A spherical cut for a stone, with a rounded surface and no facets.

Cameo A hard stone or fragment of shell or other material (for example, lava) with a design or figure carved in relief. The material is generally in more than one layer of different colors so that the design in relief contrasts with the background.

Cap A functional component shaped like a hemisphere, in glass or metal, with a hole for stringing and with a primarily decorative function.

Carnelian A mineral with a reddish yellow color belonging to the chalcedony group of the quartz family.

Cavallotto A "bridge-shaped" unit with a decorative function. Sometimes it is functional when used as a link between two other decorative elements.

Celluloid A transparent, flammable, light plastic with a pearlized patina composed of plasticized nitrocellulose and camphor. Although invented in Great Britain, it was patented in America by two brothers, James and Isaiah Hyatt, and widely used in the 1920s for making combs and bangle bracelets and so forth. It is used to imitate ivory, bone, coral, pearls, and tortoise shell.

Centrifugal casting A technique of casting molten metals in molds that are rapidly rotated by a centrifuge in order to force the liquid substance to adhere to the walls of the mold.

Ceramic A paste of clay, chalk, or kaolin and water that is shaped, dried, and baked in a special oven at high temperatures. Used for making porcelain, majolica, terra cotta, and other similar materials.

Chain A functional, and in some cases also decorative, component composed of links looped through one another.

Charms Good luck or souvenir pendants.

Chatelaine (Fr.) Decorative plaque worn at the waist on which work implements (keys, scissors, watches, whistles, seals, thimble holders, needle cases) and toilet articles (perfume bottles) were hung from chains. Very popular from the 17th century to the early 19th century. It also refers to a certain type of brooch.

Chisel Pointed implement for chiseling metals.

Chiseling Metalworking using chisels for creating decorative designs on jewelry.

Choker A slightly graduated short necklace fastened about the neck like a collar. In French, *collier de chien*.

Clasp Functional component equivalent to a device for closing and opening a piece of jewelry; sometimes also serves a decorative function.

Clip Similar to a brooch, but has a hinge type of clasp.

Cloche (Fr.) A woman's hat with a bell-shaped brim.

Cloisonné (Fr.) An enameling technique in which the design is constructed on the surface with metal or wire strips, filled in with colored enamels, and then fused.

Cold-enameled (see *Painted*)

Collar A necklace worn at the base of the throat.

Convertible A piece of jewelry that can be taken apart to create other objects, such as a necklace whose clasp can be detached, thereby becoming a brooch.

Coral Calcareous secretion of marine organisms, with an arborescent structure, in colors from rosy white to red. Often used as beads for necklaces.

Craquelé Refers primarily to ceramics, majolica, and paintings, suggesting a "cracked" surface. The cracks either occur naturally because of a lack of elasticity in the object, or they can be induced by a particular technique.

Crystal Glass in which the stabilizers have been replaced by lead oxides endowing the glass with a special quality of luster, purity, and brilliance.

Crystal stones Faceted imitation stones made from crystal. They have more sparkle than glass stones, though one cannot tell with the naked eye whether a stone is glass or crystal.

Cultivated pearl A real pearl produced by human intervention. A small bead of mother-of-pearl is inserted as an irritant into a live pearl oyster, which then isolates it and covers it with a calcareous substance. The oyster is then thrown back into the sea for a period of three to seven years, during which time the pearl is developed.

Cut steel Steel studs with numerous facets.

Demi-parure (Fr.) A group of two or three of the four pieces of jewelry that make up a whole parure.

Déposé (Fr.) A word impressed on the back of jewelry (real, costume, or couture) made in France whose design has been filed with the appropriate agency in order to protect it from being plagiarized. In English, design patent.

Design patent A certificate of the paternity of a design or decoration which is protected against imitations for a certain number of years. In French, *déposé*.

Die A mechanical implement made of tempered steel that is impressed with the shape of the object to be reproduced.

Doublé d'or (Fr.) A laminate obtained by pressing a thin leaf of gold onto a metal plate (usually copper).

Earring An ornament for the ear. As regards the shape, it can be:
button
drop or pendant
hoop
As regards the fastener, it can be:
clip
pierced
screw back

Electroplating The process of immersion in a galvanic bath, as the result of which a thin gold, silver, or rhodium-colored layer forms on the object that has been immersed. If the layer of gold plating is less than 0.0007 of an inch, it is called a "flash," if greater, the object is said to be "plated."

Elephant hair Treated elephant hide was primarily used in the 1920s and 30s for creating filiform ornaments broken up with insertions of gold leaf.

Embossed Refers to a surface with "bosses" (protruding parts) in relief. Different types include rough, smooth, or diamond-work embossing.

Embossing Process in which the chisel is used on the back of an object in order to create a decoration in relief on the surface.

Enameling (see also *Guilloché, Cloisonné, Basse taille, Painted*) Glass, reduced to a powder, is suspended in water and placed in prearranged cavities in the metal. It is then heated in an oven and melted. The glass powder is colored by adding metal oxides. Enamels can be opaque or transparent.

Engraved Refers to a surface carved

GLOSSARY

with a burin in order to obtain an ornamental design.

Faceting Cutting a stone using a grindstone in order to obtain different shapes, called facets, on the surfaces of the stone.

Fastener The upper part of the pin, generally bar-shaped, on whose back side the clasp is welded and which generally serves as a "fastener" for a pendant.

Festoon necklace A short necklace with a design that tends to be broader in the middle than at the sides.

Field (of the mark) The shape of the space within which a mark is impressed.

Filigree A type of metalwork made by interlacing metal wires and soldering them to one another (typical of the workmanship in Hobé costume jewelry) or to an underlying metal surface, as seen in many of Fahrner's jewels.

Fineness (of precious metals) Ratio of the weight of precious metal contained in an alloy to the total weight of the alloy. For silver, it is generally expressed in thousandths. Examples include: 800 silver means that out of a thousand parts of alloy, 800 are silver and 200 are of another metal; 925 silver (or sterling) means that out of a thousand parts of an alloy, 925 are silver and 75 are of another metal; 18 carat gold means that in a gold-based alloy, expressed in twenty-fourths, 18 parts are gold and 6 are of another metal; 18 carat gold is the equivalent of 750 gold, as out of a thousand parts of an alloy, 750 are gold and 250 of another metal.

Foxtail chain A chain made of flat, close rings so as to form a surface that resembles dense fibers.

Galalith A plastic obtained from casein with plasticizers added to it. It is hot-pressed and hardened through immersion in a solution of formaldehyde. Frequently used for making small objects.

Gallery A functional component, in metal or plastic, composed of a perforated surface on which decorative elements are "embroidered" using beads and perforated stones.

Galuchat Dyed skin of a ray. Widely used in the Art Deco period as an ornamental material for its colorful appearance, with nuances of varying intensity.

Girandole Type of hanging earring in vogue in the late 17th century and 18th century. The earring was embellished with three or four drop-shaped pendants made so that they would move with the wearer's every movement.

Glass paste A pulp of crushed glass that is colored by adding metal oxides. The resulting mixture is annealed to yield a type of opaque glass, widely used, especially for French jewelry. In French, *pâte de verre*.

Gold filled (see *Doublé d'or*).

Grinding An operation carried out with a grindstone, a rough-edged tool composed of a revolving, abrasive disk or a revolving disk of felt with paste and abrasive sand; used for working metal or glass objects.

Guilloché (Fr.) Transparent enamel that covers a surface decorated almost always by machine; more rarely, hand chiseled.

Hallmark The mark required by the laws of individual countries to identify and guarantee the fineness of the precious metal employed. It can be a number, a symbol, or an abbreviation and varies from country to country and in different periods of history.

Hammered A metal surface showing the marks made by a hammer in order to create a rough surface.

Hardstone Semiprecious stones that have an opaque color (turquoise, carnelian, opal), generally used in making mosaics.

Horn Organic material derived from the horns of certain mammals, which, when heated and pressed, was widely used to create ornaments in the Art Nouveau period.

Imitation jewelry Jewelry executed in semiprecious or common metals and imitation stones made from glass, that deliberately copies real jewelry to the greatest degree possible.

Imitation stones Faceted stones made from colored glass imitating precious and semiprecious stones.

Injection molding Thermoplastic materials are injection-molded using a technique similar to pressure molding (the melted material is injected into the mold).

Inlaid Surface decorated by inserting either fitted pieces of metal or other substances like ivory into the metal that makes up the object, in order to create ornamental motifs.

Ivory Natural material, usually obtained from elephant tusks, which is cream-colored, ductile and elastic, and has been used since antiquity for small sculptures, engraved pieces, and for small objects and ornaments.

Jais (Fr.) Imitation jet, heavier and colder to the touch, drawn from black faceted glass paste. In English, French jet.

Jet Black variety of coal found primarily in Whitby, England. It becomes extremely glossy after extensive polishing. Its glass imitation, a specialty of the French and Bohemians, is called *jais*, or French jet. Widely used in jewelry of the Victorian era, it was originally worn as a sign of mourning.

Lamp bead A bead obtained by melting a glass rod over a flame.

Lapis lazuli A mineral of the sodalite group, known since the time of the Persians, blue in color and dotted with gold resulting from inclusions of pyrite in the mineral.

Lariat A necklace with decorations at the ends of the strand. It is tied in a knot instead of being closed with a catch in the middle.

Locket A circular or oval pendant designed to hold a picture, memento, or the hair of a loved one.

Lost-wax casting After making a wax model of the desired object, it is covered with plaster or calcium sulfate, leaving one spot free which acts as an orifice. When the covering has hardened, the wax is melted and flows out of the opening into which the liquid metal is then poured.

Lucite A type of hardened acrylic; a transparent plastic used to simulate rock crystal, patented in America in 1941.

Malachite A mineral composed of basic copper carbonate with an intense green color, used as an ornamental semiprecious stone and, when reduced to a powder, as a pigment to color lacquers.

Marcasite A compact, brilliant mineral with a dark gray color, composed of oxidized iron. It can be cut like a precious stone and is generally mounted on silver. Widely used to make shoe buckles in the Edwardian Era, when marcasite took the place of the cut steel used up until that time.

Metal mesh A fabric fashioned from thin wires or minute units of metal.

Metal plating The metals from which costume jewelry pieces are made are covered with precious metal both to protect them from oxidation and to make them look similar to precious metals (gold and platinum). The metals can be gold-plated, silver-plated, or rhodium-plated with a thin layer of gold, silver, or rhodium by means of a galvanic bath.

Minaudière (Fr.) A small evening bag.

Mold In founding, a handmade structure into which molten metal is poured in order to be shaped.

Moonstone (also called "adularia") A mineral of the feldspar family with a white and milky-blue color.

Mother-of-pearl The white, iridescent inner surface of the shells of a variety of mollusks, used to make buttons, buckles, and other decorative elements.

Mounting The technique by which precious or nonprecious stones are secured.

The varieties of mountings are innumerable and differ according to their historical period. The principal types include:

    bezel (a strip of decorated metal wound around the edge of the stone. Primarily used for cabochons and round-cut stones)

    nonvisible (generally used for the main stone and set in such a way as to appear invisible)

    pavé (very closed mounting of stone similar to a pavement-like effect)

    prong and claw (whereby the stone is secured by small strips of metal. The crown setting is made with only a few prongs. The coronet is used for a round setting. The claw is used for square settings)

ring shaped (the setting covers only the base of the stone, leaving the crown free)

tubular (when a setting ending in an eye is strung to form clusters of stones)

Nickel A white metal used for alloys and special steels and for plating a variety of objects.

Nickel silver (or German silver) Alloy of copper (50%), nickel (20%), and zinc (30%) used for making ornaments and cutlery.

Niello A technique for decorating the surface of a piece of jewelry, generally silver, that entails filling in designs engraved on the metal with a hot amalgam composed of a variety of substances and called, in fact, niello.

Nitrocellulose Basic component of organic origin used in making celluloid.

Onyx Black-colored mineral belonging to the chalcedony group of the quartz family.

Opaline An opaque glass obtained by the addition of opaquing agents to a glassy mass.

Oxidation The effect ensuing from the chemical action of oxygen on certain metals, causing them to lose their luster.

Painted Refers to American costume jewelry that has been colored with acrylic paints; the resulting effect is similar to cold-enameling.

Parisian chain The thin chain on which beads for sautoirs are strung. It serves as a strong support for the substantial weight of the beads. It is also used because it is very easily attached to the clasp and requires little labor. This type of chain requires larger holes in the beads.

Parure An ensemble of a necklace, bracelet, earrings, and brooch made from the same materials and with a common shape and coloring.

Parurier Manufacturer or vendor of costume accessories for women's clothing (buttons, buckles, hair ornaments, and costume jewelry).

Patent A certificate from an authorized agency stating the paternity of an invention and the owner's exclusive rights to the economic benefits derived thereof.

Patina In reference to metals, it is more correct to use the word "oxidation," which indicates the darkening of the original color. Gold becomes redder, silver darkens to the point of becoming gun-metal gray in color.

Pearl essence (also Essence d'Orient) A compound of substances derived from fish scales, cellulose, and acrylic resins for covering the surface of simulated pearls to make them look real.

Pendant A movable ornament hanging from a chain or from the fastening of a brooch.

Pierced Refers to elements of different shapes and sizes that may be strung on thread, wire, etc.

Plaque de cou (Fr.) A flat ornament of metal, stone, or other materials, with a rectangular or square shape, placed in the center of a choker.

Plastic (see also *Bakelite, Celluloid, Galalith, Lucite, Acrylic resin, Rhodoid*) A substance with a high molecular weight that becomes pastelike upon heating and can be molded to form a variety of objects. Thermosetting plastics are those which, once formed, cannot be liquified and reshaped. Thermoplastics, on the other hand, are those substances that when subjected to high temperatures can be repeatedly softened and cooled so that they can assume a desired shape time after time.

Punch The tempered steel rod used to mark metal with an image, abbreviation, number, or inscription. It is also the word for the mark imprinted by the rod.

Quartz The most common of the minerals. It occurs as large transparent crystals that are colorless when pure. There are many varieties and kinds of quartz.

Raffia A tough fiber obtained from specific types of plants that grow in Africa and in the American tropics; used for embroidered or braided pieces.

Rhinestone chain A chain composed of metal units connected to one another by joints. A rhinestone is mounted in each unit.

Rhinestones Small, colorless, faceted

glass stones. Larger faceted stones may also be called rhinestones, but it is more appropriate to use the term "imitation stones."

Rhodoid The commercial name for the thermoplastic resins derived from cellulose acetate.

Rivet A connecting element similar to a nail.

Rivière (Fr.) A type of necklace introduced in the 18th century formed from precious stones, in particular diamonds, mounted separately. In reference to stones, it means a row of graduated stones mounted individually.

Rocaille (Fr.) A style distinguished by wavy lines and whimsical shapes, rich in decorative elements (shells, small rocks, multicolor stones), resulting from stylized organic ornamental designs.

Rock crystal A variety of colorless, transparent quartz widely used in jewelry making.

Rolled gold (see *Doublé d'or*)

Rondelle A functional as well as a decorative component, pierced for stringing, with a round shape in metal, plastic, or glass, generally used as a spacer for a necklace.

Roses montées (Fr.) Rhinestones cut into a rosette (so-called because the stone obtained from this cut looks like a rosebud; the upper part is shaped like a pyramid, and the lower part has a flat base) and mounted on cup-shaped settings devised so that a strand can be passed through them.

Satinized or dulled An opaque surface with small incisions obtained by using steel brushes rotating at high speed.

Sautoir A long necklace that often descends below the waistline. When this term is used today, it generally means the long pearl necklaces of the twenties.

Semiprecious metals:
 gold laminate or a sheet of gold made to adhere to a sheet of metal, such as copper, by means of a press. The laws of different countries provide for an obligatory hallmark for silver (800, sterling, 935), while gold laminate is often not marked.

In the United States, gold laminate bears the words "rolled gold" or "gold filled."
 silver, which, depending on the area of origin, can be 800, 925 (sterling), or 935 thousandths silver.

Semiprecious stones The term generally applied to stones other than the precious ones (diamond, ruby, emerald, sapphire, and pearl). They are divided into mineral groups: beryl (including aquamarine), topaz, jade, zircon, spinel, garnet, opal, tourmaline, chrysolite, turquoise, quartz (an enormous family which includes citrine, rock crystal, and aventurine), chalcedony (agate, onyx, and chrysoprase), and the feldspars (which include moonstone, amazonite, labradorite, malachite, hematite, and lapis lazuli). They can also be of organic origin, derived from animal or vegetable substances: amber, coral, jet (fossil resin), ivory, and tortoise shell.

Setting A functional component; a seat composed of a metal cavity or surround into which stones are inserted. Each of the multitude of possible shapes and sizes of a stone corresponds to a specific setting. A setting may be "open" (with an open background) or "closed" (with a closed background). See also *Mounting.*

Simulated pearl A plastic or glass pearl imitating a natural marine pearl. It can be either round or baroque.

Snap link A functional component generally used as a clasp in the form of a metal hook with a small spring lever.

Soldering Joining of two or more metal components by a soldering alloy whose melting point is lower than that of the metals that are to be soldered.

Souvenir jewelry A piece of jewelry (in precious, semiprecious, or humble materials) created in a particular tourist destination and using local materials and traditional techniques of craftsmanship.

Spacer A functional component of both real and costume jewelry that serves as a space between various decorative elements.

Stamping The making of a pattern in

relief on metal or plastics. Today, commonly mass produced.

Synthetic stones Artificial stones whose physical, optical, and chemical properties correspond to those exhibited by the natural stone they are meant to imitate.

Tailored jewelry A type of ornament in gold-plated or silver-plated metal without stones.

Tassel Ornamental piece formed of multiple strands of silk, cotton, or other materials joined at one end. In jewelry, it was especially fashionable in the 1920s and 30s, and again in the 1950s.

Tinsel A small, twisted strip of gold or silver for embroidery.

Tombac A metal alloy with an appearance similar to that of brass, also called "fake gold," composed of 80–90% copper and 10–20% zinc.

Topaz In jewelry making, the word topaz refers to a variety of citrine quartz with a yellow to gold color. In actuality, topaz is a fluoriferous aluminum silicate that crystallizes as heavy, prismatic crystals, which are brittle and hard and come in a wide variety of colors—yellow, orange, azure, and violet.

Torchon When referring to a necklace, it means that multiple strands are entwined to form a twisted cord.

Tortoise shell A natural material, derived from the shells of tortoises. Hard and translucent, with a light yellow to dark brown grain, it has been used since Roman times to make small decorative objects and ornaments.

Trademark The sign used by a manufacturer to mark his or her own merchandise or products in the marketplace. The trademark may be the name or the initials of the maker, the name of the manufacturing company, or it may be a design or symbol. With costume jewelry, the manufacturer's trademak is generally stamped on the piece itself or on a plate soldered to the object.

Tremblant A decorative element soldered to a spring (on a brooch, a pendant, and so forth) that causes it to move slightly when worn.

"Triple-fired" baking and gold-plating Decoration applied on ceramics that have already been shaped and have undergone two baking processes: the first to make the "crust" and the second to crystallize the object.

Turquoise A hard blue stone in varying shades, most commonly a pale sky blue, deep sky blue, and greenish.

Venetian-glass seed beads Small beads cut from a glass rod.

Vermeil (Fr.) Gilded silver.

Vinyl A chemical substance derived from ethylene and used in industry for producing vinyl resins.

White metals Metal alloys with a white coloring widely used in jewelry making, containing 75% copper and 25% nickel.

Wound-glass beads Lamp beads made so that they look as if they were wound into a ball; the molten glass is pulled and wound around a metallic rod or wire.

BIBLIOGRAPHY

Alferj, P., and F. Cernia. *Gil anni di plastica*. Milan: Electa, 1983.

Becker, V. *Art Nouveau Jewellery*. New York: E. P. Dutton, 1985.

———. *Fabulous Fakes*. London: Grafton Books, 1988.

Buri, S. *Jewellery 1789–1910*. 2 vols. Suffolk, England: The Antique Collector's Club Ltd., 1991.

Davidov, C., and G. Redington Dawes, *The Bakelite Jewelry Book*. New York: Abbeville Publishers, 1989.

Farneti, Deanna C., ed. *Jewels of Fantasy*. New York: Harry N. Abrams, Inc., Publishers, 1992.

Gabardi, M. *Gioielli anni '40*. Milan: Gruppo Giorgio Mondadori, 1982.

———. *Gioielli anni '50*. Milan: Gruppo Giorgio Mondadori, 1986.

Mulvagh, J. *Costume Jewelry in Vogue*. New York: Thames & Hudson Inc., 1988.

Proddow, P. *Hollywood Jewels*. New York: Harry N. Abrams, Inc., Publishers, 1992.

Rizzoli, Eleuteri L. *Gioielli del Novecento*. Milan: Electa, 1992.

Shields, J. *All That Glitters*. New York: Rizzoli, 1987.

Stancliffe, J. *Costume and Fashion Jewellery of the Twentieth Century* in "The V & A Album." London: De Montfort Publishing Ltd., 1985.

JEWELRY INDEX

GENERAL INDEX

GENERAL INDEX

PHOTOGRAPH CREDITS